I deeply appreciate the courage Ian Britza has demonstrated in bringing the topic of disloyalty to the surface. As ministry leaders, we all deal with this. Most of the time we've swept it under the rug. Ian Britza has pulled out the rug, exposed the problem, and given us the practical tools to overcome it.

Pastor George Pearsons
Eagle Mountain International Church
Fort Worth, Texas

The Absalom Spirit

REVEALING DISLOYALTY'S PLAN
TO DESTROY YOU AND THOSE YOU TRUST

by

Ian M. Britza

Harrison House

Tulsa, Oklahoma

08 07 06 05 04   10 9 8 7 6 5 4 3 2 1

The Absalom Spirit:
Revealing Disloyalty's Plan To Destroy You and Those You Trust
ISBN 1-57794-460-7
Copyright © 2004 by Ian M. Britza
Ian Britza Ministries
P.O. Box 1606
Fremantle, 6959
Western Australia

Published by Harrison House, Inc.
P.O. Box 35035
Tulsa, OK 74153

Dedication

I have sometimes reflected on the thought that perhaps I have been given the ministry and the anointing of a needle to the body of Christ. Of course, when one's ministry and presentation of the Word of God are as challenging and thought provoking as mine have been, the dedication required can expend a demanding toll on one's family and loved ones.

Therefore, I want to dedicate this book to my two sons, Timothy and Michael. Over the years they have witnessed the disloyalty of ministers, staff members, and friends toward their father. They have heard with their ears and seen with their eyes things that would have caused many people to turn their backs on the Lord and the leaders He sent to serve and support them in building their ministry. Adding to this demoralizing predicament, they have seen the separation of their mother and father. With enough hurt and offense to cause many to turn their backs on God's call, Timothy and Michael have continued to love and honor the Lord, their parents, and the house of God. They have experienced rejection because of their father's ministry experiences and actions, yet their hearts and eyes are still focused on the Lord Jesus Christ and remain open and tender towards the things of God. I am so proud of them and want them to know that without their constant personal love and support during these last few years, my heart could easily have become embittered and disillusioned.

During the most difficult period of my life, Michael and his precious wife, Jessica, gave me a pen with this inscription: "You can do it. We believe in you." Well, my children, I will do it—with God's help.

Just as Paul wrote a heartfelt affirmation to the Corinthian church in 2 Corinthians 3:2, so I give my sons this honor: "Ye are our epistle written in our hearts, known and read of all men." Timothy and Michael, you have embraced the principles of your father, and this tells me that my heritage is safe within your hearts. May God receive all the praise, honor, and glory for your continued tenderness, sensitivity, and compassion towards the issues that are close to His heart. I am truly a proud, respected, and honored father of two sons who have now passed the test of loyalty and become true men of God.

Contents

Contents

Foreword

BY HAPPY CALDWELL

Disloyalty is a manifestation of the devil himself. Therefore, this book by Ian Britza should be on your must-read list.

Everyone either has experienced a spirit of disloyalty in the past or will have to deal with it in the future. Jesus experienced it at the hand of Judas. The apostle Paul experienced it from his most trusted associates and in his writings to Timothy revealed that "Demas hath forsaken me, having loved this present world.... Alexander the coppersmith did me much evil: the Lord reward him according to his works" (2 Tim. 4:10,14).

Having experienced disloyalty in his own life and ministry, Ian Britza takes the highroad of forgiveness but at the same time issues a warning for the rest of us. Let us recognize the signs of disloyalty in our own ranks so we can avoid the destructive nature of Satan in our own lives and in our ministries.

We have but a short time left to fulfill Christ's assignment in our lives and ministries; therefore, we must train up leaders to avoid the destructive spirit of disloyalty.

Pastor Happy Caldwell
Agape Church
Little Rock, Arkansas

Foreword

BY DON CLOWERS

Ian Britza is a great man of God, a man of impeccable character and integrity. When he has been challenged by unusual circumstances, through storms and adversities in life, he has never surrendered or retreated but has always remained focused on Jesus Christ, his Savior and Lord, and stayed faithful and loyal to his call.

Many people have been hurt or betrayed by those they have loved and trusted. Many times this causes people to put up walls and never learn true faithfulness and loyalty. When you have been hurt and betrayed, you must confront it and deal with it. You cannot run from it. You must receive healing. Remember: The way you leave a relationship or church is the way you will enter another.

This book deals with the issues of the heart, and I trust that as you read you will say, as David did, "Search me, O God, and know my heart..." (Ps. 139:23). As you read this book, examine your heart and determine that you will never be caught in Satan's trap to be in rebellion, which would cause hurt and pain to yourself and others.

I believe that if you will read this book with an open heart and mind, God will help you to be a loyal person, blooming where you are planted and allowing Him to promote you into your destiny.

Reverend Don Clowers
Grace Family Church
Dallas, Texas

Acknowledgments

The material within these pages has come from numerous pastors and ministers who have spoken into my life, and men and women whom I have been profoundly honored to minister to and pastor.

Certain people come to mind whom I need to acknowledge for the wisdom and friendship they have imparted to me. Each of these people has experienced disloyalty at one time or another but has continued to stay in love with Jesus and forgiven those who have been disloyal.

Brother Kenneth Copeland has profoundly influenced my life with the message God has given him to preach to this generation. I have been blessed, encouraged, and inspired by the decision he has made to walk in love with those who have come against him over the years. I desire to follow his example as the Word of God instructs us in Hebrews 6:12: "Be...followers of them who through faith and patience inherit the promises." He has truly experienced the joy and satisfaction of walking in love towards his brethren, and I intend to follow his example.

Pastor Bob and Joy Nichols have been my spiritual parents for over fifteen years. In 1988, Pastor Nichols took me under his wing, and I became his spiritual son. Pastor Nichols took the place of my father, who is in Christ's presence, and I have been able to enjoy the delights of being a loved, corrected, nurtured, and trusted son. Dad and Mum Nichols mean the world to me, and I have learned so much from their example as individuals, pastors, and leaders of leaders. Most of all, I have learned from watching their wonderful and ever-growing love for each other. I acknowledge the tremendous influence that they have imparted in my life, and I will continue to receive the consistent and continual affirmation that comes from their hearts to mine.

Pastor George Pearsons of Eagle Mountain International Church has been a precious friend for many years. We have spent many hours sharing our hearts, our dreams, our failures, our aspirations, and our successes with each other. He is an example of a truly called, anointed, and appointed New Testament pastor. His love and tenderness for the people whom God has called him to pastor is a delight to observe and an example to imitate.

Pastor Happy Caldwell has been my friend and colleague for many years. At a crucial time in my life, Pastor Caldwell and his precious wife, Jeanne, gave me the prayer, support, and encouragement that was critical to my continuing what God had called me to accomplish in my nation. Pastor Caldwell once said, "There comes a time when you just have to get out there and lead, so go and do just that: Lead." It was Pastor Caldwell who expressed confidence in the material now in this book and encouraged me to write it. Thank you, Pastor Caldwell, for your belief and trust in me.

At a significant period in my life, Dr. Mark T. Barclay came alongside me and said, "I believe in you, Ian, and am not ashamed to stand beside you." I am indebted to him in ways that I cannot adequately express. He is a man of honor, integrity, and principle. Dr. Barclay's counsel as a friend and colleague for over twelve years has given me the wisdom to close the door to many decisions that would have hindered the call on my life for years to come.

For nearly twenty years, Bishop Harry Westcott has been a father, a colleague, and a precious friend to me. I know no other person who has faced disloyalty more than this precious man of faith, yet he continues to share God's healing words with hundreds of hurt people from his ministry headquarters on the edge of the Outback. From me he has withheld nothing, sharing things that would only increase the call of God on my life. He has not been deterred by those who are unwilling to face the impossible; rather, he strives for an adventure in faith. May his legacy of faith live in my heart and life.

Dr. Margaret Court has been a cherished friend for almost twenty years. I have lost count of the many times I answered the phone, and there was her voice. She has continually encouraged me, constantly striving to show me what God could do with a person who is completely committed to His plan. She has never held back anything that has needed to be said. I trust her integrity and the principles she lives by and encourages in others. I am deeply grateful for the friendship we have cultivated over the years.

I want to express my gratitude and appreciation to the rest of the Britza family and their children: my brothers, Murray and Ross, and their wives; my sisters, Joy, Vivien, and Karyn, and Karyn's husband. Beyond all that they have heard, perceived, seen, and read, they still believe in me and the call of God on my life. Many a minister has been ruined by the opinions and illegitimate judgments of their families, but I am blessed to have a family who desires to be a part of what God has called me to fulfill in my nation. I am sure our parents, Reverend Bill and Beryl Britza, would have been proud of us. May we continue to pass on their heritage to our children and children's children.

I would like to express my appreciation to J.P. and staff of the Starbucks outlet at North Richland Hills in Fort Worth, Texas. I refined most of the manuscript at this location, and I so valued their support and good humor.

Finally, I would like to acknowledge Jesus, without whom I most certainly would have been a mess, especially these last four years. He has kept my heart soft, tender, and open to new friendships and relationships. I have had marvelous opportunities to be offended, hurt, greatly disappointed, and shattered, but the Spirit of the Lord has always been present as I have looked to Him for new paths, friendships, and opportunities. May God truly receive the glory from what has been expressed in these pages for the benefit of the body of Christ worldwide.

Introduction

I have devoted my life to preaching and teaching God's Word. I have pioneered new ministries, bringing together men and women and inspiring leaders of other ministries around the world to do the same. Through all the years that I have done such work, one constant obstacle has remained: disloyalty.

Even the best of ministry teams can come to grief from internal politics rooted in disloyalty. As a pastor and ministry leader, I have made every effort to protect my people from this divisive enemy. Just as God has taught me from the Word, I have trained my staff to use biblical tools to stay free from the temptation of disloyalty.

Now through this book, I want to impart to you the same lessons God has taught me. Whether you are a pastor, a minister, part of a ministry team, or a church member, this book is for you. The wisdom God has imparted to me can now be yours to use to resist the spirit of disloyalty.

Disloyalty is not a new problem among God's people. In fact, the Bible contains many stories of godly people who became disloyal. All too often people who once served God with a whole heart became infected with the spirit of disloyalty. This spirit influenced them to such a degree that, even though they may have started with the purest of intentions, they became disloyal and committed acts they never before would have dreamed of.

The spirit of disloyalty has brought harm to many individuals who have set out to serve God. With hopeful beginnings, everyone overtaken by the spirit of disloyalty has ended up fighting against the very One they once claimed to serve.

Consider what happened to Aaron and Absalom, great leaders in the Old Testament, when they succumbed to the spirit of disloyalty. Aaron bowed to the pleading of the Israelites and allowed them to worship idols while his brother Moses was on Mt. Sinai in the presence of God. The young and proud Absalom stood up against his father, King David, and was willing to plunge the entire nation into a civil war in order to fulfill his selfish desires.

The spirit of disloyalty has been at work in the earth since the fall of Lucifer and his entrance as Satan, and it has continued throughout history. In fact, the history of Israel is a classic illustration of disloyalty. Generation after generation turned their backs on such great leaders as Moses, the prophets, and even God Himself. In the New Testament, even Jesus had to contend with one of His most loyal friends.

Today, we can be sure that leaders are subject to similar levels of disloyalty. Therefore, we must find a solution. The call and the vision of God are too high a price to pay for failing to learn how to protect ourselves and our ministries from disloyalty.

If, like me, you have invested many years into raising up a strong ministry leadership team, you might consider yourself disloyalty-proof. The thought that one of your closest supporters could turn on you may be far from your mind. You may feel that you share a common vision with your co-laborers. Perhaps you do not see any disharmony in the ranks. Nevertheless, without warning, disloyalty can plunge into your ministry and disintegrate what you have worked so hard to build.

In the pages that follow, you will learn the origin of disloyalty, its danger signs, and how to expel it before it infects you or your ministry team. You will learn not only how to handle damage control if disloyalty strikes, but also how to prevent dissention from ever infiltrating your team.

Whether or not you have experienced the heartbreak of disloyalty, this book will help you understand how God wants your ministry team to function for the success of His kingdom here on earth. The truth of this message will keep your team loyal and free from the devil's divisive schemes.

If the devil has already invaded your life with disloyalty, you are not alone in your pain. I have experienced the hurt and profound disappointment of seeing and hearing people I loved, pastored, and trusted turn with venom, disrespect, dishonor, contempt, and insolence towards me. I have been accused of doing things that were so abominable and repulsive to me that I have just sat down and cried until, like David's men at Ziklag, I had no more tears to shed. I have lost the friendship of precious co-laborers in ministry. I have had my motives and principles questioned, laughed at, and mocked. Those to whom I have given my life and anointing have called me a hypocrite.

Yes, I know what it is like to be in the merciless grip of disloyalty. However, after losing everything I considered dear, I have heard the Spirit of God quietly whisper to my heart, "I have new and precious people to bring into your life to bless and honor you, and you in turn will honor and speak into the lives of countless people. I, your God, will call you blessed."

God has shown me how to keep my heart soft and tender, to reach out once again, to make a connection with those He wants me to love and pastor, and to receive their love and support as well. I need to stay in love with God and His people, and so do you. My prayer is that through this message, you will be truly blessed and your heart and your ministry will be forever free from the spirit of disloyalty.

CHAPTER 1

Loyalty: God's Design for Friendship

In order to understand the devastating effects of disloyalty, we must first realize the great value of loyalty in our lives. The richest soil God gives us for planting and developing seeds of loyalty is friendships. We develop loyalty in us toward our friends, but of equal importance is developing loyalty in our friends toward us.

In our friendships, the ultimate potential in each relationship is to develop the fruit of the Father's loyal friendship toward us.

In *Matthew & Mark: A Relational Paraphrase,*[1] Bible scholar Ben Campbell Johnson interprets the following words of Jesus as relating to this vital part of our lives—human friendship:

Jesus said:

> "*The farmer sows the word. Some people are like seed along the path, where the word is sown. As soon as they hear it, Satan comes and takes away the word that was sown in them. Others, like seed sown on rocky places, hear the word and at once receive it with joy. But since they have no root, they last only a short time. When trouble or persecution comes because of the word, they quickly fall away. Still others, like seed sown among thorns, hear the word; but the worries of this life, the deceitfulness of wealth and the desires for other things come in and choke the word, making it unfruitful. Others, like seed sown on good soil, hear the word, accept it, and produce a crop—thirty, sixty or even a hundred times what was sown.*"

MARK 4:14-20

The richest soil God gives us for planting and developing seeds of loyalty is friendships.

In addition to paraphrasing Mark 4:14-20, Johnson also shares his interpretation of this passage: "Here's the explanation. The planter plants an authentic witness of God in every relationship...."[2] In other words, every time we meet someone new, God plants a witness of Himself in our lives. Therefore, when we meet someone for the first time, we should be sensitive to what the Holy Spirit wants to do with us in that relationship.

However, each of us responds differently to the initial introduction, and this is where the seeds of eventual disloyalty can plant their destructive crop. Johnson continues: "Planting on the hard earth is like an encounter with a person whose response to the witness is superficial; thus, there is no penetration of his defenses. Immediately, the Adversary snatches away the impact of the encounter."³

Every one of us has met people described in this passage. They are the ones who, when you meet them, immediately begin to look for other people to talk to. I have observed this behavior at every minister's conference I have attended. Admittedly, I have likely displayed this kind of attitude, and I must acknowledge that I have hurt myself by being inconsiderate towards those who have sought my attention and even friendship.

I venture to say that each of us has responded to the possibility of friendship with disinterest. However, this kind of attitude prevents loyalties from beginning. It also disables a person's leadership, because a good leader is able to celebrate and communicate with people of all categories.

Therefore, we do well to not only gravitate toward people who appeal to us on a surface level, but to open our hearts to the deeper substance of each person we meet. The following comments on verse 16 warn against looking only at people's surface qualities:

> Those persons who are represented by the thin layer of
> earth are those who immediately celebrate an encounter with

an authentic communicator of God. But the joy is short-lived
because they do not open their inner being to the presentation
of the Spirit, and soon the surface encounter withers.[4]

I know what it's like to be the target of this attitude. In some churches I have been enjoyed and celebrated for surface reasons, such as my Australian accent. However, when the anointing manifests and I minister the Word, sometimes people forget the initial enjoyment because they don't like the feeling of the Holy Spirit's conviction. Suddenly, in those times, I have been seen as a liability rather than a blessing. Though they have enjoyed my surface qualities, they have failed to receive the deeper substance God placed within me.

Many people look at the surface issues of the people they meet and, as a result, fail to receive the full potential of the encounter, as Johnson expresses in his comments on verses 18 and 19:

> *Those seed sown among thorns are like encounters with*
> *people who are possessed with wealth or pleasure, whose*
> *awareness is on externals, and these and other interests*
> *quickly erase the impact of the encounter.*[5]

Several years ago at a minister's conference, a pastor of quite a large congregation introduced himself to me and inquired about the size of my congregation. When I told him, he stood back, a little surprised, and became rather indifferent. When I asked him what was wrong, he said, "Why are you invited to speak in such large churches when your church is so small?"

Like this man, many ministers think invitations to preach come on the basis of the size of one's congregation. Sadly, these people have completely missed the picture, failing to see that what matters is loyalty, relationship, and the condition of one's heart. In fact, on one occasion I asked a precious pastor why he was comfortable asking me to preach, and he answered, "I trust your heart, Ian."

Too often, people look for friendships with others whom they think can benefit them because of their financial status, geographical location, similar interests, physical appearance, friends, and accomplishments. What a shallow idea it is to base friendships, relationships, and destinies on superficial qualities, when each person we meet has the potential to be a friend.

On the other hand, have you ever met someone with whom it appears you have already made a deep connection? The following comments explain what takes place in such meetings:

...what matters is loyalty, relationship, and the condition of one's heart.

> The seed sown on good ground are those encounters in which there is a real meeting of persons, those in

which each feels himself or herself to be met by God. These seed then are received, they grow and bear fruit—some thirty, some sixty, and some a hundred times as much as the initial planting.[6]

I believe the experience described in this passage is a meeting of kindred spirits. This is one of the most precious incidents in life. I am thankful to have had the joy of such meetings several times over the years.

A well-known preacher once said, "You are a wealthy man if you have three precious friends in your lifetime." In my opinion, this statement underestimates the potential God gave us for friendship. According to this passage, God brings countless men and women across our paths—some to just speak into our lives, others to become a vital part of our lives.

Sadly, many of us have experienced the disloyalty of those whom we thought God had brought into our lives. Then, because of their hurtful and insensitive actions, we have pulled back and become overly cautious instead of reaching out to new friendships.

Jesus said in Mark 4 that the seeds are to grow and produce some thirty fold, some sixty fold, and some even one hundred fold. If we apply this principle to friendships, then we can see that we are to produce countless friendships that are kindled and lighted by the Holy Ghost. Therefore, I believe that we must resist the temptation to withhold ourselves from embarking on new and treasured friendships.

If the spirit of disloyalty has attacked your life, destroyed friendships, and broken your heart, I encourage you to open your heart to the touch of the Holy Spirit and your mind to the possibility of new friendships. Your new colleague or friend may be the one whom the Holy Spirit has been preparing for you all along, so do not miss your opportunity to discover God's design for a loyal friendship.

If you feel you have enough friends already, I encourage you, as well, to open your heart and mind to the possibility of new friendships. Some men and women keep their close friends in a tight circle around themselves. They are friendly to others, but they only allow their established friends to be close to them.

While I understand the desire to allow only a small group of friends to come near and the instinct to protect your heart from becoming close to others, I have to ask what Jesus would do. I wonder whether He would prevent someone from coming into His close circle of friends if that person had the same kindred spirit that the others around Him had.

My question is whether we are sometimes too selfish with our friendships, being unwilling to share them. My advice is to consider your attitude toward your friendships and the possibility of new ones, and follow your own conscience. God may be waiting for you to open your heart so that He can reward you with the gift of another loyal friend.

Several years ago, after I experienced a very difficult and demanding situation with some people in my church, I met a man from America for the first time. The Lord had been speaking to this man about pastoring a church, and he shared his heart with me about this desire. Over the years we developed a strong friendship, and the church he now pastors has grown wonderfully under his leadership. In fact, his church affects the whole world in some way on a daily basis.

Our friendship has turned into a covenant relationship and something that I never take for granted. It came after the Holy Spirit manifested an authentic witness of Himself to us. In turn, we decided to develop our friendship, which developed into a covenant relationship.

Such a relationship, one of loyalty and trust, is what God desires for each of us to have with one another. He wants us to have friendships that endure times of triumph and times of crisis. In fact, until crises occur, we do not know the quality of our friendships. It is at this point that we become aware of just how close and supportive our friendships are.

Over the last few years, I have lost very dear friends during crises. Men and women have withdrawn their companionship and fellowship from me, and in the middle of my pain I have asked myself, "Would I have done that?"

A few years ago, in the midst of a very difficult and painful period of my life, God spoke a powerful truth into my heart. I had lost the friendship of a precious man, someone with whom I had developed a strong friendship. During this painful time, I learned some important lessons that have protected me from losing my joy and allowing my heart to disintegrate into small pieces of bitterness, bewilderment, confusion, and profound pain.

When I used to teach youth about Christian relationships and dating, I would share a truth with which God had enlightened me several years before. It was simply this: "You do not qualify for a relationship until you have passed the test of friendship."

I thought the man whose friendship I lost and I had entered into a "covenant relationship" when, in fact, we had not even passed the "test of friendship." Because of his proven faithfulness on several occasions, I thought that our "loyalty" was reciprocated. As a result of his proven faithfulness to me, I did not expect him to be disloyal.

The Lord brought everything into perspective by sharing a profound truth with me which was: "You do not qualify to become disloyal until you have passed the test of faithfulness."

In my frustration, I thought of asking God to do something to my offender, though that whim only lasted a minute or two. I always knew that it was wrong for me to entertain such thoughts; I just could not understand why the pain was so great.

It turned out that God could not heal me until I set my wounded heart not at this man's feet but at the feet of Jesus. I fought this with much vigor and force, until I remembered a statement made by a minister friend of mine that I had heard over twenty-five years before: "There are only two times to say you are sorry: when it is your fault and when it is not." Finally, I rested my heart and told God I was sorry. God then began to reveal to me some truths about relationships.

Disloyalty comes from faithful, as well as unfaithful, people. It hurts the heart so much after one has expended the time, the effort, the strength, the struggle, and the finances to fortify a friendship. Sometimes this building process takes years to accomplish, and then the person confidently believes that the relationship has become a covenant friendship.

In my situation, although I had thought my friend and I were at that place of common trust, the sad fact was that he did not share my level of loyalty. The overwhelming hurt that resulted inside of me was more than anything I could bear because it came from someone I had perceived to be a faithful friend. He could not communicate with me about the situation, and we lost all the ground we had gained over the years of our friendship.

In this and other relationships, I felt as though I had shared my heart so much that those with whom I thought I had relationship knew everything about me—good and bad—and I knew nothing about them. It made me feel as though I should never again share my heart with another person. Thank God I never embraced that theory, because it would have prevented the new and precious friendships that have since entered my life.

However, I still had to deal with my heart over the issue of this man's disloyalty. I had to understand why it was so difficult to get rid of the nagging pain that manifested whenever someone mentioned him or I saw him. I'm sure we all share these reactions to disloyalty, but sometimes we just don't know how to stop them and destroy their influence in our lives.

God continued to reveal why these things were happening. He showed me that I had to stop concentrating on the other person and turn the spotlight onto my heart. I had to put my motivations on the table to be inspected by the Holy Spirit.

When I followed His instructions and laid my heart before Him, I saw the insecurity in me. Consequently, I was able to see the same in others. The Lord showed me that I needed to begin to make allowances (not excuses) for others and the way they did things. Disloyalty comes from faithful people (not only from unfaithful people) because faithful people, in their human frailty, sometimes respond out of their own insecurities instead of seeking the Lord for the way He wants them to respond.

My first act of commitment was to take communion and ask the Lord to forgive me for harboring unforgiveness towards these people. It was not easy to do.

Quite recently I had to go through this process again, and it was no easier this time. I had been accused of desiring to steal a great deal of money and also to appropriate some equipment that was thought not to be mine. What was peculiar about the situation was that the people making the assumption had known me several years and should have known my character well enough to immediately dismiss the notion.

...I needed to begin to make allowances (not excuses) for others and the way they did things.

Again, I knew God required me to lay my heart before Him and seek His forgiveness. "Why is it," I kept asking God, "that I am the one required to ask forgiveness? What about them?"

His response pierced me. He said, "Your heart is what is important to me, Ian. I have wonderful plans for you, and your responses to these matters are crucial to your fulfilling your destiny before Me."

I was not thrilled about this. I was still a little annoyed and wondered why He did not speak to me about the heart of those who had spoken against me. Out of my hurt, I even thought to myself, *This is too hard. I don't care about the call on my life or the vision or my destiny. Just give me some justice, Lord.*

However, I did eventually come to my senses. I remembered that the Lord looks upon the heart and that we are judged from our hearts. Down deep I really did not want my offenders to be hurt. They were hurt and frustrated a little themselves, and all I needed to do was to give them to the Lord and be sure I held nothing against them.

I dealt with my lost friendship at the communion table, once and for all. It was not easy to accept that he no longer wanted my friendship. However, I no longer held his disloyalty against him. And that was the victory: I had stopped disloyalty from growing and taking a foothold in my heart.

Loyalty is not always the easy route. Even in established relationships, it is sometimes a battle to keep the seeds of disloyalty and unfaithfulness from taking root in our hearts. However, it is a battle worth fighting because it will keep our hearts pure toward God and man and free from the spirit of disloyalty.

DISLOYALTY AMONG US

We live in an age in which the fruit of disloyalty abounds. Many people in this present era disrespect the principles and values that our predecessors upheld for the sake of their families, communities, and countries. One only has to look at the news to see that people have abused their right to freedom, desecrating the liberties so many men and women have given their lives to maintain and preserve.

Disloyalty is the "violation of allegiance."[7] To *violate* is "to fail to show the requisite respect for: treat or handle in a disrespectful or high-handed manner...."[8] These are prevalent characteristics of our present age.

Note, for example, the great disrespect and irreverence with which people sometimes handle their own nations' flags. Such pretense is being passed down to the next generation, some of whom can already be found alongside those who are marked by this spirit of disloyalty.

Many people enjoy the benefits of democracy but are disloyal to the foundational principles upon which it is built. The word *disloyal* means "…marked by lack of adherence to a sovereign, leader, country, principle, or cause…lack of adherence to vows, obligations, or promises especially in friendship or marriage."[9] We are beginning to see an increasing number of people of democratic nations displaying a lack of adherence to their countries, the principles upon which their countries stand, and their leaders. When exercising one of the most valuable rights of a democracy, freedom of speech, and expressing opinions that oppose those of government leaders, a citizen of a democratic government should still maintain loyalty to their leaders, adhere to them, by praying for them, speaking honorably and respectfully about them, looking for things that they can actually agree with them about, and letting them know that although they may strongly disagree with them on many matters, they honor the position they hold.

Disloyal also "indicates lack of complete faith, loyalty, and adherence to a person, cause, or country…."[10] We are witnessing a decline of faithfulness to obligations and promises, especially in friendships and marriages. Every day children observe the breakdown of the sense of importance in holding to commitments and responsibilities. We have bred a generation of people who no longer see the necessity of obeying and honoring authority.

The statistics about the number of children in my nation of Australia among whom are teenage girls who get pregnant and obtain abortions or bear children out of wedlock; teenagers who contract venereal disease, commit suicide, drop out of school, commit crimes and go to jail; children who die from the results of poverty or in car accidents, are arrested on drug or alcohol charges, see their parents divorce, or are physically and sexually abused are alarming.

We should not be surprised to see disloyalty and faithlessness in our communities when they are so alarmingly evident in the local church. In an effort to avoid offending the world, many churches have taken on its appearances and behaviors. Even our churched children see disloyalty walked out right in front of them. By the time they become adults, many have seen very few, or no, examples of loyalty, allegiance, faithfulness, or truthfulness. As a result, they cannot model these characteristics to their own generation or the following generations. The end result, if this pattern stayed its course, would be a faithless generation.

The dictionary definition of the word *faithless* has changed along with society. The meaning "not believing in God or religion" is now "archaic."[11] A faithless person is one who is "lacking strong convictions," one who is "not to be relied upon," one who does not adhere to a "pledge" or an "allegiance."[12]

Today, we have few leaders with strong convictions and principles. The low standard of excellence that our youth have witnessed in their authority figures has laid the foundation for their own low standards. As a result, many young people, tomorrow's leaders, have set aside biblical principles and replaced them with sin, saying, "If our leaders are doing it, then it must be okay."

Today, more than ever, we need to be aware of the divisive spirit of disloyalty so that we can stop it from entering our own lives and the lives of those we mentor. We need to know how God intended all of our relationships to function and, most importantly, how to walk in the light of His will for our relationships.

CHAPTER 2

The Way of Absalom

Disloyalty begins when the enemy sows his seed and it takes root in a person's heart. Nowhere is this more clearly seen than in the life of Absalom, whose story is found in 2 Samuel 13.

Absalom had a sister named Tamar. They, along with their many half-brothers and half-sisters from their father David's marriages, lived together in the royal palace in King David's City—modern-day Jerusalem. One of these half-brothers, Amnon, had an incestuous lust for Tamar and plotted with one of his cousins, an equally deviate person, to lure Tamar into his room. The plan worked, and Amnon sexually assaulted and humiliated his half-sister. Under Jewish law, Tamar was now unable to marry and therefore shamed for life. In response to this tragedy, Absalom offered to take care of her.

The Bible doesn't record whether David disciplined his son Amnon for his serious offense. We do know that he was deeply angered (2 Sam. 13:21), but the king's apparent inability to administer justice caused a rift in his family that had far-reaching consequences.

Verse 22 gives us a glimpse of one of those heart-breaking consequences: "And Absalom spoke to his brother Amnon neither good nor bad. For Absalom hated Amnon..." (NKJV). Absalom hated his half-brother because Amnon had forced Tamar and began to plot revenge on him. Absalom's pure intentions were turned to a long-term anger and hateful hunger for revenge. Verse 32 (AMP) says, "...This purpose has shown itself on Absalom's determined mouth ever since the day Amnon humiliated his sister Tamar."

Whether the king knew of the animosity that boiled in his son's heart, we do not know, but this condition went on for two years before Absalom hatched his plan. Disloyalty becomes more and more destructive with time. It grows and festers with each day that goes by. In Absalom's case, it began in his heart with the offense of Tamar's rape, and it festered in his heart until he responded with cold-blooded murder.

Now Absalom had commanded his servants, saying, Mark ye now when Amnon's heart is merry with wine, and when I say unto you, Smite Amnon; then kill him, fear not: have not I commanded you? be courageous, and be valiant. And the servants of Absalom did unto Amnon as Absalom

had commanded. Then all the king's sons arose, and every
man gat him up upon his mule, and fled.

2 SAMUEL 13:28,29

As King David mourned the loss of his son Amnon,
his other son, Absalom, ran away and hid. (v. 37.)
Absalom became a man filled with hate, anger, bitterness, and fear. In the beginning, he had simply wanted
justice. When it didn't happen, he took things into his
own hands, and that is where his problems began.

Through the course of Absalom's actions, he went
from being a protective brother to being a fugitive
member of the royal family, unable to live in his own
nation—all because he allowed disloyalty to grow in
his heart toward his father and took matters into his
own hands.

Meanwhile, if King David had been inept in
parenthood before, he was now about to fail miserably.
Although he pined for Absalom, he made no attempt
to forgive him or ask him to return home. (2 Sam.
13:39; 14:1.)

Now Absalom's heart was loaded. In addition to
hate, anger, bitterness, and fear, he now had feelings of
rejection, humiliation, shame, and complete disrespect
tearing apart his heart. In fact, it was only through a
shrewd deception schemed by Israel's commander-in-
chief, Joab, that David eventually made the decision to
allow his son to return home. (2 Sam. 14:1-22.)

21

Then, in what can only be seen as an act of delayed punishment, David announced a condition to Absalom's return: They would never speak to each other again. Second Samuel 14:24 records this edict: "And the king said, Let him turn to his own house, and let him not see my face...."

Now Absalom was an outcast in his own land. Can you imagine how he must have felt? He tolerated this treatment for the next two years and then asked Joab, who had orchestrated his return, to organize an audience with his father. He asked Joab twice without a favorable response, and then in total frustration Absalom set fire to the general's farmland to force a response.

> Then he said to his servants, "Look, Joab's field is next to mine, and he has barley there. Go and set it on fire." So Absalom's servants set the field on fire.
>
> Then Joab did go to Absalom's house and he said to him, "Why have your servants set my field on fire?"
>
> Absalom said to Joab, "Look, I sent word to you and said, 'Come here so I can send you to the king to ask, "Why have I come from Geshur? It would be better for me if I were still there!"' Now then, I want to see the king's face, and if I am guilty of anything, let him put me to death."
>
> So Joab went to the king and told him this. Then the king summoned Absalom, and he came in and bowed down with his face to the ground before the king. And the king kissed Absalom.
>
> 2 SAMUEL 14:30-33 NIV

The end result was that David agreed, perhaps reluctantly, to meet the son he hadn't seen for more than four years. (v. 33.) Although this might seem like a breakthrough for restoration, Absalom took this as a sign of approval to start acting out a new role as a pretender. The reunion with his father had not quashed Absalom's traitorous thoughts. He was now even more vehement than before, and he had a new passion–to steal the throne.

It began ever so innocently (2 Sam. 15:1-6) and was allowed to continue for four years while he secretly built up a private army and won the hearts of the common people. Then, with military precision, he struck.

It was almost ten years from the time his sister was defiled to the time he stormed into Jerusalem at the head of his army and pronounced himself king. It was ten long years during which his attitude grew increasingly worse.

The spirit of disloyalty grew inside Absalom until it consumed him. He became such a proud and evil person that in 2 Samuel 17:1-4 it is recorded that he even agreed to the murder of his own father, King David. In his mind, usurping the throne, seizing untold wealth, and becoming the most powerful man on earth weren't enough: His father had to die. That is the extreme to which Absalom's disloyalty grew, and it is the extreme to which disloyalty can grow in any person who does not deal with it quickly.

Each situation, big or small, involves right and wrong attitudes. This was Absalom's problem. Years of anger and a hunger for revenge motivated him to rebel against his father.

Many in the church have experienced this same frustration and anger within the ranks of church leadership. Working with people from all walks of life, in numerous trying circumstances, has caused some leaders to forget how Jesus would respond. Consequently, like Absalom, they take matters into their own hands, and tragedy is the result.

When I think of Absalom, I think of a man who had no one to speak into his life. He had no one in whom he felt confident to the extent that he would allow the person to correct and adjust his heart and attitude towards his own father.

Each situation, big or small, involves right and wrong attitudes.

Isolation is a terrible thing, and when David put Absalom into isolation the seeds of disloyalty grew day by day, even in the middle of Absalom's great desire to come back into his father's love, care, and attention.

Absalom could not see things clearly, and in that state it is easy for anyone to fall headlong into fear. Fear manifests when one cannot see the way out of a predicament. Then the spirit of fear causes the person to become irrational, illogical, unreasonable, and difficult.

I believe that Absalom got so frustrated with not seeing any justice that the spirit of fear compelled him to take things into his own hands. When anyone does this, it usually results in an even bigger mess. In Absalom's case, it would eventually cost his precious life.

Absalom did not start out as an irrational, illogical, unreasonable, and difficult man. He had been a wonderful young man who had the eye of his father, David. He was extremely handsome, intelligent, and gifted. He was obviously admired and accepted by the people of David's court and kingdom.

However, when he saw injustice that wasn't addressed as he thought it should be, he took things into his own hands and ultimately lost everything.

Many times people focus on issues that are not worth their energy, and ultimately lose the things that really matter. We must be sure to continually keep our hearts and minds set on those things that really matter and not

Keep our hearts and minds set on those things that really matter....

on those matters that could cost us our peace, health, family, and ultimately our destiny.

CHAPTER 3

The Disloyalty of a Close Friend

Not everyone has experienced the betrayal of a very close friend. Some have lost employees, associates, and sub-leaders, but very few have felt the merciless sting of betrayal and conspiracy at the hands of a close and familiar friend.

Imagine the devastation of witnessing an intimate friend change his or her heart towards you. Even worse would be the resulting pain if that friend wanted to help your detractors usurp your authority, destroy everything you had worked for, and assist in having you killed!

King David found himself in just such a dilemma when his friend Ahithophel, his counselor, someone whom David, a king, considered to be his "equal," his "guide" (as we see in David's reference to Ahithophel, the subject of Psalm 55:13), joined Absalom's conspiracy against him. Second Samuel 15:30-31 reveals the moment when David made the sad discovery of his friend's betrayal:

> And David went up by the ascent of mount Olivet, and wept as he went up, and had his head covered, and he went barefoot: and all the people that was with him covered every man his head, and they went up, weeping as they went up. And one told David, saying, Ahithophel is among the conspirators with Absalom. And David said, O LORD, I pray thee, turn the counsel of Ahithophel into foolishness.

Notice that Ahithophel was not a servant, not another son, and not a commander: He was someone whose counsel to David, and it was the same with Absalom, was of such reputation that it was treated as if God Himself had spoken! (See 2 Sam. 16:23 MESSAGE.) You would think such a man would understand the importance of covenant friendship, but Ahithophel abandoned David's friendship in pursuit of his death!

David had thought highly of this man Ahithophel. The two must have spent many hours together discussing the Law of God. They were likely close enough to share their hearts—their weaknesses, their joys, and their sorrows—with one another. David might have trusted in Ahithophel so much that he told Ahithophel, who was more than likely Bathsheba's grandfather,[1] how he had dealt with the issue of his sin with Bathsheba and how wonderful it was to receive God's forgiveness for the murder of her husband.

The scene may have looked like one from *Godfather III*. In the movie, the main character sits down in a solitary place with a priest and verbally sets in motion an outstanding scene where, with painful outbursts of remorse and unutterable expressions of guilt, he confesses the sins he has committed in his lifetime.

Sadly, very few of us have a friend this close.

I remember a very tender moment with a friend who had lost his child and asked if I would fly interstate to spend some time with him. I quickly agreed. Late into the night, he shared his heart and loss with me. It was a moment I will never forget.

Such moments don't come often in our lives. However, when they do come, we can walk through them far better with a friend than all alone.

We all need friends with whom we feel free enough to share not only our dilemmas but also our weaknesses. I believe this was the kind of man Ahithophel was to David. Listen to the heart of David when he shares about Ahithophel in the Psalms:

> For it was not an enemy that reproached me; then I could have borne it: neither was it he that hated me that did magnify himself against me; then I would have hid myself from him: but it was thou, a man mine equal, my guide, and mine acquaintance. We took sweet counsel together, and walked unto the house of God in company.
>
> PSALM 55:12-14

In this passage, we can sense the brokenness of a man who has been betrayed, let down, and deceived. We sense his absolute devastation, abject sorrow, and utmost disbelief and astonishment as he pours his heart out onto the page.

Right in the middle of the grief David was experiencing from the betrayal of Absalom, the news came that his trusted friend Ahithophel had abandoned him. In the very hour when he was needed most, Ahithophel broke David's heart.

I can imagine how he felt. When my marriage fell apart, I was devastated and simply overwhelmed for quite a few months. I felt forsaken by my most intimate friends. Many people later asked why I hadn't gone to them for support, but no intimate fellowship had been developed with these individuals. On the other hand, the one or two people with whom I thought I had covenant fellowship did not come to my aid or minister to me.

During those painful months, all I felt I could do was go into hiding and protect my heart from becoming hard, bitter, and resentful. I tearfully asked, "God, where are my friends and associates when I so desperately need them?" Then, in the middle of that lonely and isolated time, false accusations began to surface. I felt I simply had nowhere to turn.

Each of us at one time or another has had to deal with rejection, as David did. He called Ahithophel, "my equal, my acquaintance, my guide." This was not a new friendship, but one born through pressure and the demands of life. Ahithophel was David's peer. The *King James Version* says he was his "acquaintance," which means one who has "personal knowledge";[2] "familiarity, intimacy...";[3] a "familiar friend."[4] The Hebrew word for "acquaint," *cakan*, means "know intimately."[5] The word is only used once in the Bible and is found in Job 22:21, where we are invited to acquaint ourselves with God: "Acquaint now thyself with him, and be at peace: thereby good shall come unto thee."

It is quite clear that from David's point of view Ahithophel was a very close friend and companion. He even goes further and says that Ahithophel was a guide to him. Once again, from the Hebrew, "guide" means that he was a close and intimate friend,[6] not just someone whom David hired to be around him and serve him. "The primary sense is that of one who is always in company with another...a guide or companion or friend. As such, the companion is not expected to betray (Ps. 55:13...)."[7] To David, Ahithophel was "...a man my equal, my companion and my familiar friend" in the Psalm 55:13 wording of *The Amplified Bible*.

It is clear, then, that Ahithophel was David's friend and that David loved and respected him. It is no wonder that David expresses his pain at the news of Ahithophel's disloyalty, as we see even further in Psalm 55:20-21:

...he hath broken his covenant. The words of his mouth were smoother than butter, but war was in his heart: his words were softer than oil, yet they were drawn swords.

In this passage, as in the rest of the Psalms, David shares exactly what is in his heart. And in this situation, his heart is broken by the disloyalty of his friend. *The Amplified Bible* renders the last part of verse 20 like this: "he has broken and profaned his agreement [of friendship and loyalty]."

The Message puts it together magnificently, drawing the reader into the pathos of David's experience:

This, my best friend, betrayed his best friends; his life betrayed his word. All my life I've been charmed by his speech, never dreaming that he'd turn on me. His words, which were music to my ears, turned to daggers in my heart.

Reading this passage, we feel David's rage and suffering. We witness the tragedy of the moment. David says, "His life betrayed his word." May we never experience the shame and dishonor of having this said about us!

David was shattered by the fact that Ahithophel had broken his covenant with him. If ever a man knew what covenant was all about, David was that man! He had experienced a strong covenant with Jonathan, so he knew the value that was placed on a covenant friendship.

Therefore, when David announces that Ahithophel has broken and profaned their covenant, we know it is a very serious matter to him. To profane something is to "treat with irreverence...or contempt (something sacred),"[8] to "blaspheme"[9]—to be disrespectful and insolent about it. This is how David describes Ahithophel's response to their covenant agreement.

David continues to express his true heart in verse 22 (AMP):

> Cast your burden on the Lord [releasing the weight of it] and He will sustain you; He will never allow the [consistently] righteous to be moved (made to slip, fall, or fail).

The Message says (v. 22):

> Pile your troubles on GOD's shoulders—he'll carry your load, he'll help you out. He'll never let good people topple into ruin.

David's heart comes through with the solution for his situation: Throw it all on God; give it completely to Him. It reminds me of my father's words of wisdom when someone hurt me: "Son, if you know the truth, and God knows the truth, who else really needs to know it?" Conversations like that with my father always frustrated me because I wanted someone to hurt as I had been hurt!

David must have felt the same way. Look at the way he concluded his thoughts about his betrayers:

> But you, God, will throw the others into a muddy bog, cut the lifespan of assassins and traitors in half. And I trust in you.
>
> PSALM 55:23 MESSAGE

I can certainly identify with the pleasure he must have felt when making such a statement! However, there is no power in being offended, no victory in unforgiveness. True power lies in the wonderful gift God has given us in the ability to forgive. Only if we are born again and Jesus is our Lord can we truly forgive. Then, if we still can't forgive, we need to repent and ask for God's mercy and grace to do so.

Never underestimate the power of forgiveness. It is one of the most effective agents of healing God has given us. David practiced forgiveness—and so he should, for God had forgiven him much. In Luke 7:47, Jesus tells us that those who love much are forgiven much. What a powerful concept! We know David had a great capacity to be forgiven, so we know he must have had a great capacity to love. He knew how to love, even those who had turned so bitterly against him. He knew how to forgive, for love "keeps no record of wrongs" (1 Cor. 13:5 NIV).

God highly and favorably seeks those who walk in love as His Son Jesus walked in love while on the earth. In fact, Jesus died so that we could personally experience and walk in His love.

Because David let go of the offense of Ahithophel's disloyalty, his heart was healed. However, 2 Samuel 17:23 shows us Ahithophel's tragic end. When he realized his counsel would not be followed, he went back to his home, got his house in order, and promptly hanged himself. The scene reminds us of David's trust that God would "throw the others into a muddy bog, cut the lifespan of assassins and traitors in half." What a heart-breaking end for man who had experienced the delight and pleasure of genuine friendship.

Never underestimate the power of forgiveness.

Never put aside years of friendship over a misunderstanding: Life is too short, and friendships are too few. When you are tempted to end a friendship, what really motivates you? Second Corinthians 5:14 says, "...for the love of Christ constraineth us...." Other words for "constraineth" here are "controls and urges and impels" (AMP) and "compels" (NIV). To be "constrained" by the love of Christ is to be controlled, urged, impelled, and compelled by it; in other words, to be driven, motivated, ruled, and required by it to act. Love will always release you to do the right thing!

It's so easy to talk oneself into offense, but the major characteristic of a person of faith is walking in love—the love of God, *agape*.[10] We must resolve to walk in love with those who hurt us; we must decide to not be provoked by people. Before reading on, you may need to get on the phone with someone very precious

Love will always release you to do the right thing!

to you and simply say, "I'm sorry. Please forgive me."

I encourage and exhort you to not stand by and allow your long-term and enduring relationships to falter and weaken. In the past, I have been unsuccessful in keeping some friendships that so mattered to me. However, I have firmly decided to protect the precious gift of the covenant friendships I have been given since! With God and my friends, I will help to nurture these relationships into maturity.

Ever since I made this decision, I have made the following confession, and I encourage you to say it, too: "As Jesus continues to be Lord over my life, I am a valuable friend to the one God gives to me who needs my companionship. I am worthy of a long-term covenant friendship."

Now the battle for these friendships begins. In the following chapter, you will find the danger signs of disloyalty. Because you will know them, you will be able to stand against them and maintain the covenant relationships God is bringing into your life and ministry.

CHAPTER 4

The Danger Signs of Disloyalty

A team of any kind must run smoothly together in order to produce maximum results. This is especially true in church and ministry leadership. Therefore, we must keep our minds clear of anything that would turn our leadership against itself.

Disloyalty is a state of mind. Because we have the ability to decide what goes into our minds, we can reject the spirit of disloyalty. It simply requires that we continually purify our thoughts, our motives, and our attitudes by the Word of God.

Left unchecked, however, the spirit of disloyalty will start to take root in our hearts. As the root of disloyalty grows, it reveals a number of key danger signs that can alert us to the possibilities of future conflict. Each sign is an opportunity for us to stop and reject this spirit before it finally consumes and destroys us.

STEALING HEARTS

One danger sign is that disloyal leaders try to steal the hearts of the people. In 2 Samuel 15:2, Absalom stood in a convenient place to turn the hearts of the people against his father, the king. In Jewish culture, it was common for legal matters to be addressed by the city's leaders at the main gates. However, King David was absorbed in other activities, so Absalom took his place.

Absalom used this position of authority to begin spreading disloyalty and speaking out publicly against his father. (v. 4.) He created a power base to support his plans for the future.

A pastor, minister, or leader may not be handling things properly—he may even be in sin—but to use this as an excuse to usurp the influence of one's leader is to follow the spirit of disloyalty. There is never a right time to steal hearts. The Bible gives specific guidelines for addressing sin in church leaders, and we will explore this topic in depth in a later chapter.

PROMOTING SELF

Another danger sign of disloyalty, as we've seen in Absalom, is self-promotion. In the passages we've studied, it is interesting to note that in order to cast aspersions on another (King David), Absalom was fixing the spotlight firmly on himself.

Clearly, pride, ego, and selfishness eventually expose themselves when a person's heart is increasingly consumed by disloyalty. God tells us in Psalm 101:5 (NKJV) that the proud will fall: "...a haughty look and a proud heart, him I will not endure." Furthermore, James 4:6 makes it clear that "God resists the proud..." (NKJV).

Driven by a desire for their idea of justice, retribution, or retaliation, disloyal people intentionally defame people of importance who might stand in their way. They become wrapped up in their own importance and enter the self-promoting phase of disloyalty.

In this phase, people desire to attract attention. They want a pat on the back, for example, in front of the church body. Members of any leadership team need to remind themselves that they are there to help build the ministry and make sure the vision is being fulfilled, not to receive the accolades of men and women and most certainly not to take over.

BEING PRIDEFUL

Pride, another danger sign of disloyalty, is a mighty weapon of the enemy. So many times throughout the

Word, God warns us to beware of this destructive force. With pride, Satan can charge right through a person's defenses and stir up ill feelings of disunity.

Pride will cause a person to pursue personal ambitions regardless of the mission or vision of the leadership team. It will cause a person to focus on one's own plans—and the ministry will come second. The phrase "hidden agenda" certainly relates to people in the growing stages of disloyalty.

BEING EASILY THREATENED

Disloyal people think highly of themselves and are threatened when their ideas are not used. Absalom perceived that his father was a weak leader. Absalom seemed to think that if King David couldn't run his own home properly, he himself could govern a nation better than his father could. This belief in his own abilities over those of the king helped turn him into a rebel and a traitor.

In ministries, God gives the vision to the leader, and it requires faith to believe the leader is hearing from God. At the same time, there is no reason why people under leadership cannot share their ideas; however, that is where it should be left. If their initiatives are not taken up, they should not become threatened or hurt.

When rejection of an idea is taken personally, disloyalty can step in.

HAVING AN INDEPENDENT SPIRIT

Another danger sign of disloyalty is an independent spirit. God calls us to work together and be a team— not to be independent, self-reliant, self-sufficient, unconstrained, or detached.

Independent people do not want fellowship. They separate themselves. They are hungry for position and recognition. They want to be treated just like the leader, enjoying the same courtesy, respect, and honor.

However, respect is earned, not handed out. Consumed by their own ambitions, disloyal people cannot see that it is God who promotes. When He decides to raise someone up, it is at the best time and for the right reasons, and it produces good results.

For example, in Genesis 41, Joseph went from being a prisoner to being the prime minister in one day because God was in control. However, self-induced promotion (usurping the leader's authority) is always for the wrong reasons and can only produce confusion, division, fear, hurt, and death to any ministry.

...it is God who promotes.

JUDGING GOD'S ANOINTED

Another danger sign of disloyalty is judging God's anointed. Disloyal people not only fail to submit to leadership, but they judge and criticize them.

We can see from the Scriptures that it is very dangerous to affront God's anointed. For example, Jezebel's attempt to kill the prophet Elijah led to her violent death. (1 Kings 19:1-3; 21:23; 2 Kings 9:30-37.) Similarly, after King Saul spent years trying to destroy God's anointed, he suffered a gruesome death, along with his sons, his armor-bearer, and all of his men. (1 Sam. 31:1-6.)

NOT BEING ABLE TO TRUST

Another danger sign of disloyalty is the inability to trust. Absalom knew before he could act that he had to secure one important response from his potential followers—complete trust. This is why he invested so much time standing at the city gates, probably shaking hands and kissing babies. He had to build a bridge of confidence that would cause ordinary Israelites to turn away from their faith in the man who had led them from victory to victory and ushered in a time of prosperity and peace.

Even though Absalom had disloyal motives, he understood a very important leadership principle, one that is true even today. Whether it is in heading up a team or leading a church, a leader must have trust. Without it, he or she can achieve nothing as a leader.

Nowhere is this more apparent than when a pastor or church leader is in the midst of a decision-making process over the future direction of the ministry. Growing ministries face decisions daily. This is often a time when people's trust in their leadership is tested. It is not uncommon for change to spark fires of disloyalty.

When complete trust is demonstrated, the congregation acknowledges that the leaders do not have to share the whole picture with them. They do not demand to know all the details from which the pastor has drawn his conclusions.

However, in order for a ministry leader to gain trust from his people, he must be able to show toward them the same quality of trust he requires from them. Many people have had leaders continually ignore their suggestions, plans, submissions, and proposals. Perhaps they have kept their hearts pure and continued diligently serving the minister of God, yet without respect for their faithfulness.

Countless precious servants of God are caught in the trap of not being trusted by their leaders in ministry. I know of a youth leader, for example, whose pastor only observed negative characteristics in his energetic and spontaneous personality. The pastor did not trust that he was flowing with the leadership or the church, planning enough, being consistent, or running with the church's vision.

What the pastor seemed to fail to realize was that most youth leaders see things differently than their pastors do. In order to minister to the specific needs of the youth, they *need* to see things differently. Nevertheless, with mutual trust, the hearts of leaders can be united even if their methods are different.

Even if a pastor sees negative characteristics in a church leader, he can deal with them by meeting with that leader and developing his skills. Only a secure minister can do this. He cannot be one who constantly battles with insecurity in his own call, position, title, and giftings.

In churches and ministries where insecure ministers lead, no one can do anything creative without the leader first coming up with the idea.

When I was pastoring in the early years, I had some insecurity-driven characteristics in my leadership method. Sadly, I discovered too late that because of my insecure behavior I had squandered relationships with precious men and women whom God had sent to assist me and I them on the paths to our fulfilled destinies.

If you are a team member in a place in which you find it difficult to fulfill what you have been designated to achieve because you are not trusted, you must keep your heart soft and open and *always* think the best of your leader. If your motives are still being questioned, you need to make a change if you desire to grow, mature, and develop. Respectfully make an appointment with your leader, share your heart, and ask for his blessing to leave and find a ministry with which you can work.

...the hearts of leaders can be united even if their methods are different.

It would not be wise for you to stay in that place and cause strife or unwittingly cause anyone to doubt the leadership. God always supports the pastor in a church or the leader in a ministry, unless that person is in sin—a problem addressed in a later chapter. Even then, God will still love and support His called and anointed minister. In an instance given in Psalm 105, the Lord, speaking of the Israelites, "...suffered no man to do them wrong...Saying, Touch not mine anointed, and do my prophets no harm" (vv. 14,15).

In 1 Samuel 24, we see that even though King Saul was clearly in the wrong, David was not going to "touch" him because he was still the king and the Lord's anointed leader. David said, "...The Lord forbid that I should do this thing unto my master, the Lord's anointed, to stretch forth mine hand against him, seeing he is the anointed of the Lord" (v. 6). Therefore, it is important that we trust our leaders and remain pure in heart toward them. I cannot recall having very many problems with my leaders in the past, and I think that was due to my servant's heart, which came through in my behavior toward them and my prayers for them. Never forget the power of prayer. If you pray genuinely for your pastor, minister, or leader, one of two things will happen: Either you will change, or he will. Most of the time it will be you.

Exodus 32:1 shows us a matter of trust. Moses, having to lead many hundreds of thousands of unarmed people through hostile lands to their homeland, sought divine wisdom from God. When Moses climbed atop Mt. Sinai to receive God's instruction for their future, the people whined, "He's gone!" and plummeted into disloyalty. Tragically, Aaron allowed them to step into this sin.

In light of this example, do not pressure your leader. Pray that God will give your leader the insight and confidence to follow the path that God has prepared. Also, have patience. Change does not always happen overnight. In fact, it rarely does.

Put your trust in God and in your leadership. Pray for them. Stand in faith for them, and submit to what they bring you.

BE WATCHFUL

Never forget the power of prayer.

The danger signs of disloyalty are important to know and recognize—in yourself and in your leadership team. It's important to watch for them and deal with them as soon as you see them. Left to grow, the spirit of disloyalty will only consume and destroy. Therefore, be watchful—not suspicious, but watchful in the spirit— of the danger signs of disloyalty.

CHAPTER 5

Handling Disloyalty in Your Midst

Lucifer demonstrated the first act of disloyalty, and his actions led to his excommunication from heaven. Isaiah 14:12-14 reflects on the event:

> How art thou fallen from heaven, O Lucifer, son of the morning! how art thou cut down to the ground, which didst weaken the nations! For thou hast said in thine heart, I will ascend into heaven, I will exalt my throne above the stars of God: I will sit also upon the mount of the congregation, in the sides of the north: I will ascend above the heights of the clouds; I will be like the most High.

Lucifer's example shows us that an organization born of strife can only produce strife. What is born of God will remain, and what is born of Satan and strife will be destroyed. In New Testament terms, this is the principle of sowing and reaping. (Gal. 6:7.)

In light of this truth, critics of ministers should never believe that they can take over a ministry from its rightful leader and then start anything with a pure motive. A ministry born of strife breeds strife. On the other hand, a ministry born of loyalty breeds loyalty, and such a ministry will produce good fruit in its community, city, and nation.

When strife is found, it is critical that it be handled properly. Moses was wise in his handling of the strife in the Israelite camp and of Aaron's sin. Though Aaron's disloyalty allowed the Israelites to commit the abominable sin of idolatry, Moses wisely forgave and restored him. As a result, rather than becoming a hateful outcast, Aaron accomplished many things as an associate leader of the nomadic Israelite nation.

As a modern-day example, years ago I read that a well-known soft drink company launched a new drink that became an expensive failure. The top marketing associate left in disgrace. However, a while later, in a spirit of humility and grace, the corporation rehired him, which allowed him to become successful in other projects.

...a ministry born of loyalty breeds loyalty, and... will produce good fruit....

I recently heard another modern-day example of a leader restoring his subordinate after a major mistake. It is about a test pilot who was flying a new type of plane. While airborne, the plane's engine stalled and the plane plummeted toward the ground. With much struggle, the pilot successfully brought the plane back up and to base—where the mechanics discovered that it had been given the wrong fuel! Rather than chastise the guilty mechanic, the pilot chose to let him keep looking after his plane. As a result, the mechanic became an efficient and trusted member of the pilot's ground crew for many years to come.

All of these examples represent leadership decisions that brought about unity and restoration. In every situation, every leader needs to make the right decisions about the people who serve them. When people are highly critical of them or make major mistakes that harm the ministry, leaders must choose to either let them go without strife or nurture them.

It is important for leaders to remember that team and congregation members are imperfect, just as leaders are imperfect. As leaders, we will always be able to find fault in those we lead. However, we must remember that God chose our teams and ultimately wants them to take part in His plan.

Let me ask you a question that is well worth answering honestly before God: Do you have the patience and tolerance to ignore unjust criticisms and simply continue with the vision and goals that the Lord has given you? If the criticism is coming from outside of your realm of influence, then you need to make a quality decision to listen only to the voice of God. If, however, the criticism is coming from a ministry leader under your authority, it may be necessary to remove such a person from a position of responsibility.

It is never easy to do this, especially if the person is a friend. It is even more difficult if the person in question has been in a high profile role and others are more supportive of the person than they are of you.

Depending on the circumstances surrounding the dismissal, you will not necessarily gain support for doing what you believe to be right. However, it is important that you follow your heart and not allow disloyalty to infect more people.

Disloyalty in your ranks may come as a shock to you. I am sure David was completely taken by surprise when his own people took up arms and marched on his city. However, nothing comes as a shock to God. He knows the hearts of your leaders, and He can give you divine wisdom to deal with them.

Simply continue with the vision and goals that the Lord has given you.

Remember: You are not supposed to handle the problem alone or in your own strength. Give it to God. The supernatural power of God can work in any crisis and cause you to exit the crisis in a better position than when you entered it.

HOW TO PROPERLY DISMISS A LEADER

In my years of ministry, I have discovered some helpful steps for properly dismissing a leader. I have listed them here to benefit you, the reader, in the event that you should find it necessary to remove a disloyal team member from leadership.

1. Deal with the situation in private. Satan will want to unsettle everybody. Do not let him. Keep the disloyalty private.

2. Have witnesses with you.

3. Document the person's inappropriate behaviors, and keep records of all meetings and phone calls. This material can be used to support your case if it ever reaches litigation or hits the news media.

4. Depending on the circumstances, you might elect to explain the issue to the church after everything is resolved. This should prevent the guilty party from later sowing seeds of dissent.

In the best case scenario, the disloyal person in your midst will have a change of heart and express genuine remorse. In this case the person could be

*...God can...
cause you to exit
the crisis in a
better position
than when you
entered it.*

reinstated. It is best to let the person seek repentance in private after his own process of self-examination. Therefore, I do not advise chasing after the person, but letting the person return.

If the person does return, it is wise to retest the fallen leader. He or she does not have to be restored immediately to the former position of leadership. The last thing a ministry wants is a disloyal spirit reentering to cause a second rebellion.

CHAPTER 6

Disloyalty-Proofing
Your Leadership Team

It is important that we know how to get rid of the spirit of disloyalty in our midst. However, it is even more beneficial to know how to keep disloyalty from ever entering our hearts or our ministry teams. Following are some practical steps you can take to disloyalty-proof your leadership team.

TRIAL PERIOD

The first step you can take is to have a trial period for people who could potentially become a part of the leadership team. This is not always possible because of the immediate need that you may have to fill leadership positions. However, it is vitally important to know a little bit about a person's character before giving the person leadership responsibilities.

Unfortunately, because of their great need for assistance, many pastors decline the opportunity to screen people who want to serve in their churches. If the leadership from the church from which a person comes cautions against the immediate use of a person, it would behoove a minister to heed that counsel until the person has at least confirmed some stability and integrity. If a potential servant shows no commitment, the ministry most likely does not need him.

TIME

The second step to disloyalty-proof your leadership team is to increase the amount of time you spend with your department heads. In order to find fulfillment in the task of leading a department, your leaders need enough time with you to discuss their departments, their goals, their problems, their successes, and their breakthroughs. In fact, this step is one of the most effective ways to disloyalty-proof your ministry. Money cannot pay for the results you would get from increasing your time with your own leaders.

JOB DESCRIPTIONS

The third step to disloyalty-proof your leadership team is to have job descriptions written out for each member of the team. Of course, this takes time. However, it is wonderful thing when those under you know exactly what they are required to fulfill. Do your own homework, and be sure you are as thorough as you can be. This will instill confidence in your people and let them know that you are genuinely interested in their department and have studied their vision and dream of what they want to accomplish.

SAY "THANK YOU"

The fourth step to disloyalty-proof your leadership team is to always be quick to say "thank you." I like what Proverbs 3:27 says: "Withhold not good from them to whom it is due, when it is in the power of thine hand to do it."

Saying "thank you" can prevent many problems and elicit positive results. It does not take much effort, but it can create a powerful response. A word timely spoken can be the catalyst for great achievements, but a word left unsaid could be the destruction of a life.

57

BE A SERVANT

A word timely spoken can be the catalyst for great achievements....

The fifth step to disloyalty-proof your leadership team is to be a servant. One of my spiritual fathers, Pastor Bob Nichols, is a wonderful example of a servant in leadership. He never leaves anyone's presence without saying, "Is there anything I can do for you?"

A few years ago, when a tornado ripped through downtown Fort Worth and destroyed Calvary Cathedral International, a friend called Pastor Nichols and asked how he could assist him. The friend, Pastor George of Eagle Mountain International Church, let him know that he could use the Eagle Mountain church facility while his congregation stabilized.

After thanking him, Pastor Nichols said, "Pastor George, is there anything I can do for you?"

In the middle of his crisis, he was asking what he could do to assist someone else. That is what a true pastor does. He has a servant's heart and is willing to serve at all times.

DO NOT CONDEMN FAILURE

The fifth step to disloyalty-proof your leadership team is to not condemn failure. Nothing is more humiliating and embarrassing than for personal failures to be made public. First Peter 4:8 (AMP) says, "...love covers a multitude of sins [forgives and disregards the offenses of others]." As leaders, we should be the examples of showing tenderness and forgiveness even in the most dreadful of mistakes and blunders. We should do this because we ourselves make mistakes.

CHAPTER 7

Disloyal Leaders

Not only staff, department heads, and church members can be disloyal, but leaders can as well. The secular world offers plenty of examples of disloyal leaders. Disloyal political leaders have exploited their positions to pursue personal pleasure and gain. Disloyal corporate leaders have taken their money out before their companies have gone bankrupt, leaving the workers financially destitute with nowhere to turn. Of course disloyalty, in some sense, pervades the entire secular world.

However, as we have seen, disloyalty can also be found among God's people—even among His chosen leaders. The Bible is filled with illustrations of disloyal leaders. Consider, for example, the stories of Aaron, Samson, King Saul, and Judas.

Aaron's disloyalty led him to make an idol for the newly rescued Hebrew nation while his brother Moses stood before God awaiting His instructions for the people. When confronted about his sin, Aaron said, "I told them, 'Whoever has any gold jewelry, take it off.' Then they gave me the gold, and I threw it into the fire, and out came this calf!" (Ex. 32:24 NIV). His disloyalty had made a fool and a liar of him.

Samson's disloyal leadership was similarly destructive. In fact, it led to the death of many of his peers and followers. It also brought about the disgrace of his parents and family and the public ridicule of the God whom he served.

Disloyalty caused King Saul to abdicate his God-given authority over the nation of Israel. In his insecurity, he thought everyone—especially his son-in-law David—wanted to kill him. His life exemplifies the depths to which one falls when disloyalty runs its course in a person's life.

Because of disloyalty, Judas's life was destroyed. Jesus' inner circle so trusted their fellow disciple Judas that no one even thought to check up on his illicit bookkeeping. Just as in most cases of disloyalty, only after the fact were Judas's disloyal actions discovered.

There are many more examples in the Bible of disloyal people in positions of leadership, and the problem has not gone away with time. Today, most of us have respected certain leaders only to discover that they were disloyal. For example, they may not have kept their word. They may have dismissed employees and abandoned friendships because of minor disagreements. They may have failed to reward faithfulness and loyalty. They may have publicly shared confidential matters.

In whatever way it manifests, disloyalty from leaders causes far more damage than disloyalty from followers. Consider, for example, the destructive nature of disloyalty in ministers. While disloyal ministers are few and far between, their disloyalty can challenge the trust of many. Not only can it cause people to strongly question the disloyal ministers themselves, but it can challenge their faith in the truths and principles all ministers share—even their faith in God.

Furthermore, disloyalty from leaders can destroy the leadership potential in those they lead. One pastor I served would consistently remove leaders from their positions if they disagreed with him. He offered no opportunity for repentance or growth, no instruction, no training, no correction. He just showed them the door.

A disloyal leader has no desire to correct and train. He expects his subordinates to know his heart and meet his expectations. I was a praise and worship leader in a church where the pastor did not know what he wanted; however, he knew what he did not like.

Countless times I was in his office being reprimanded for not doing the right thing, but when I asked him what he wanted he could not tell me.

Similarly, another pastor placed me in the position to pastor the youth and gave me a set of tapes on a particular subject that he wanted me to teach. After several months, he told me I shouldn't be teaching the subject anymore. I wanted so desperately to be loyal to him, but I did not know what he wanted. I could see that his method of leadership was causing disloyalty among his staff, but I continued to love him as a son ought to love his father.

When his marriage broke down and he left the ministry, many people and leaders were disillusioned and some have never recovered. Thankfully, my eyes had always been on Jesus; nevertheless, his fall deeply saddened my heart. I wept all night when the news came of his decision to leave the ministry.

WHEN A MINISTER IS IN SIN

The ultimate disloyalty a minister can show toward one's people is to be disloyal toward God by knowingly living in sin while claiming to be His servant. In such an instance, it is the responsibility of those who know of the sin to respond. However, before doing so, they must know which steps to follow.

When a minister is in sin, the Scriptures very clearly detail the appropriate response. We must never take these measures lightly. So much damage can be done in a ministry if the response is not made according to the divine order of scriptural accountability. Following are the steps that need to be considered before making any decision to act on such a delicate matter.

PRAY

As I have noted, a leader's disloyalty can deeply and tragically affect his people. Therefore, in such a sensitive situation as when a leader is in sin, it is of utmost importance that the knowing individual pray before acting. Then the individual can become close enough to the heart of God to respond just as He would.

SEEK RESTORATION

We know that God is a merciful God who desires restoration. Therefore, this is an indication of how He would like us to respond when a brother or sister in Christ is in sin. Galatians 6:1 says:

> Brethren, if a man be overtaken in a fault, ye which are spiritual, restore such an one in the spirit of meekness; considering thyself, lest thou also be tempted.

...God is a merciful God who desires restoration.

One translation says, "...you who live out of the Spirit can assist him to recover."[1] Another takes it further and says, "...[who are responsive to and controlled by the Spirit] should set him right and restore and reinstate him, without any sense of superiority and with all gentleness...."[2]

The knowing individual needs to have an attitude that seeks restoration long before he goes to the leader privately and certainly before exposing the sin publicly. Realistically, it is not easy to put down the desire for justice in pursuit of God's desire for ultimate restoration. However, it is our responsibility to reflect God's nature and obey His Word even and especially when it is not easy.

I once had a situation in which a fellow minister, with whom I was in relationship, counseled a couple in leadership in my church to leave my church. My first reaction was profound disappointment and frustration with the minister and the couple. For several weeks I intensely desired to see that minister censured and reprimanded by his ministry.

I was not afraid to confront him, but my heart was not right. I did not want him to say he was sorry; I wanted him to feel the pain I had felt—and maybe a little worse.

Just a few days later, the Spirit of God said to me, "Ian, you can confront him about what he has done to you—but only if you intend to save his friendship." I had not been prepared for that, and honestly it frustrated me even more.

However, God had exposed my heart. I realized I was not in a spiritual position to bring correction because my desire was not to set him right, restore him, and reinstate him. I knew my motives had to change.

After just a week, I was ready to confront him, but with the desire to save our friendship. When I called him and shared my heart with him, he was instantly apologetic. He admitted that what he had done was wrong and asked me to forgive him. I did forgive him, and our relationship was saved.

JESUS' INSTRUCTIONS

In addition to praying and seeking restoration, we can follow three specific guidelines that Jesus gave for addressing anyone who harms us in general. As we have seen, disloyalty from a leader is certainly harmful to the followers. Therefore, when we read these words of Jesus, we can apply them to our course of action when a leader is harming others with disloyalty in the form of sinful conduct.

> Moreover if thy brother shall trespass against thee, go and tell him his fault between thee and him alone: if he shall hear thee, thou hast gained thy brother.
>
> But if he will not hear thee, then take with thee one or two more, that in the mouth of two or three witnesses every word may be established. And if he shall neglect to hear them, tell it unto the church: but if he neglect to hear the church, let him be unto thee as an heathen man and a publican.
>
> MATTHEW 18:15-17

Go to the Offender Privately

First, Jesus said that the person being harmed—in this case, the individual who has seen the offense—is to go to the offender privately.

Take Witnesses

Second, if the offender disregards the knowing individual, who is certain of the facts, then the individual is to take one or two witnesses with him. Sadly, many individuals go wrong at this step by choosing witnesses with a bias against the offender. The knowing individual needs to take witnesses whom the offender respects and loves. It is best if the knowing individual chooses a leader or a deacon, as this communicates a pure motive toward God and the offender.

Go Before the Church

Third, if the offender has not listened in the presence of the witnesses and there is strong irrefutable evidence of his offense, then Jesus says to take the matter before the church. Very few churches are structured to do this; however, this is the way our Master instructed us to deal with any serious sin within the church family.

PAUL'S INSTRUCTIONS

Paul also gave specific instructions about addressing possible sin in leaders. He made it very clear that we need to be cautious and thorough in the process.

Have Reliable Witnesses

Paul said that before bringing an accusation against a leader of the church, we need at least two or three witnesses of the person's questionable act: "Against an elder receive not an accusation, but before two or three witnesses" (1 Tim. 5:19).

One translation says, "Don't listen to a complaint against a leader that isn't backed up by two or three responsible witnesses."[3] The key word in this statement is *responsible*. A *responsible* witness is accountable and readily recognized as dependable, trustworthy, and reliable. This is a mature person whose relationship with Jesus is established, whose commitment to the church is unquestionable, and who is in good standing with the church congregation.

When preparing to confront a person's sin, we must be sure that the witnesses of that sin match this scriptural description. They must be ones who can be trusted so that when the time comes to take the next step, it can be taken with confidence and integrity.

Go Before the Church

The following verse shows us the next step: "Those who sin are to be rebuked publicly, so that the others may take warning" (1 Tim. 5:20 NIV). While this verse uses the word "publicly," I believe it is referring to the audience of the church body. I do not believe this verse calls us to make such a matter public before the secular community. I think it is best to keep these matters within the church family. This shows that we care about restoration, not just our idea of justice.

GO TO THE CHURCH ELDERS

Furthermore, we should never share our concern about a pastor, minister, or leader with other members of the congregation. Wisdom determines that it is so astute and prudent to at first approach a responsible leader in the church before even bringing up the matter with anyone else. I believe that 1 Timothy 5:20 implies, in principle, that we should go to another leader when dealing with a leader. This is why Paul stated that we are to be careful in bringing an accusation against a leader, and that the accusation had to be accompanied by two "reliable" witnesses. If the leader we approach does not listen, then we must be careful to whom we speak. Otherwise, our words could easily be construed as bringing strife and dissention into the church.

HAVE PURE MOTIVES

Above all, we must ask ourselves this question: "Am I prepared to save this friendship and begin this matter with a pure and tender heart?" This will keep our motives sound, pure, and honorable before God and before the people who will be questioning our motives themselves.

We must be careful not to steal the hearts of the people of a church or ministry. If we witness sin in our leaders, we must never privately put our case before a congregation. If we do, others could think we are trying to gauge the reactions of the people to whom we are speaking.

Anyone who has been part of a church takeover is on serious ground when trying to defend or uphold this course of action. Unless the leadership crisis is a moral, family, or financial concern, the pastor or leader has the right to correct the matter first. I believe that God clearly upholds the position of the pastor and leader.

I have heard horrible stories of people in churches conspiring to remove pastors or leaders, doing alarming things to bring their plan to fruition. May God have mercy on them, for the Bible says clearly, "...A man reaps what he sows" (Gal. 6:7 NIV).

No matter what a leader may have done or said, few will have ever actually planned and premeditated their improper course of actions or expressions of the heart. Pastors and leaders are just like you: They feel, and they hurt.

In His mercy, God designed our response to leaders' sin to bring healing rather than further pain to the leaders themselves, to the church, and to the community. Therefore, when confronting disloyalty in leaders, our goal should never be to cause deeper hurt but to bring about restoration. To do so is to demonstrate loyalty to God and to our leaders.

C H A P T E R   8

Leaders Need Fathers

One reason why ministry leaders are disloyal is simply that they have no accountability, which comes not from peers but from spiritual fathers.[1] I once heard a statement that aptly differentiates between the two: "Peers compete, but fathers correct and discipline." The leaders of today need fathers.

God's Word is designed to produce freedom and joyful abandonment. In fact, James 1:25 refers to the Word as "the law of liberty." However, in order to experience liberty, one must be made accountable to the Word. This is why biblical principles are so vital and imperative.

We have a precious principle in 1 Peter 5:1-3 (MESSAGE), in which a spiritual father gives detailed instruction to church leaders:

> *I have a special concern for you church leaders. I know what it's like to be a leader, in on Christ's sufferings as well as*

God's Word is designed to produce freedom and joyful abandonment.

the coming glory. Here's my concern: that you care for God's flock with all the diligence of a shepherd. Not because you have to, but because you want to please God. Not calculating what you can get out of it, but acting spontaneously. Not bossily telling others what to do, but tenderly showing them the way.

If Peter gave these instructions to the leaders of the early church, we can be sure that we need spiritual fathers to speak into the lives of our church leaders today. If we leaders will take this principle to heart and be sure to connect with spiritual fathers, we will nullify any chance of disloyalty creeping into our lives.

A pastor once shared a quote with me from a well-known preacher that succinctly explains why we need accountability: "It's not if you get off track; it's when you get off track" that you really need a father to come alongside to protect and minister to you.

We need spiritual fathers because they instruct us in order to build us up inside. They assist us in the development of our character—of our integrity and honor. Because they have experiential wisdom with which to offer us guidance, fathers train us how to respond to various life situations with the right course of action.

Spiritual fathers are not interested in their own agenda but only want to see their sons succeed. On the other hand, a disloyal leader wants all the credit for all the successes in his establishment. He does not genuinely want to help with the requirements for achieving these accomplishments. He seems to think leaders have been promoted from getting dirty anymore.

I remember reading about a famous World War II general whose soldiers loved him for this reason. He not only talked big but he sometimes got on the frontline with them. Likewise, a spiritual father will demonstrate by his actions the diligent effort it takes to make an establishment work.

A person will follow a father who gets down with him in his mess in order to help him get out. We can see that Paul was this kind of father when we read the following passage he wrote to the Corinthian church:

> I'm not writing all this as a neighborhood scold just to make you feel rotten. I'm writing as a father to you, my children. I love you and want you to grow up well, not spoiled. There are a lot of people around who can't wait to tell you what you've done wrong, but there aren't many fathers willing to take the time and effort to help you grow up. It was as Jesus helped me proclaim God's Message to you that I became your father. I'm not, you know, asking you to do anything I'm not already doing myself....
>
> 1 CORINTHIANS 4:14-16 MESSAGE

If you are a ministry leader or if you desire to be one day, do you have a father like this? Do not try to build a ministry without the covering of a father. If you do, your ministry will be ineffective. However, you will always have authority if you are under authority.

Dave Chislom, a good friend and pastor, shared with me that he was grateful to have a spiritual father because he could check his leaders for "ticks and fleas." I've chuckled over that statement several times, but it bears much truth. A spiritual father can help you build a sound leadership team and can help you ensure that your ministerial relationships remain strong.

One of my spiritual fathers especially helped me understand why relationships are so important. Pastor Don Clowers shared this powerful truth with me: "Every time you give your history or relationships away, you are gambling on your future." We live in an age in which people discard friendships like used coffee cups. If they disagree with something that their friends say or do, then they discard them and look for another.

I have felt the pain of having my friendship discarded. Had I not had a father to turn to, I would most likely have accepted the lies of the devil and never trusted my peers again. However, the biblical principle of being account- able to a spiritual father saved my heart from becoming defensive and closed to new relationships.

SONS HONOR THEIR FATHERS

Spiritual fathers have the duty and privilege of speak- ing into their sons' lives, and spiritual sons immediately respond with an attitude of respect, honor, admiration, high esteem, and appreciation. We can see this kind of attitude in Old Testament sons Joshua and Elisha.

Joshua sought Moses' heart because he wanted the spirit that was on Moses. Elisha had the same desire to be like Elijah, whom he actually called his father. (2 Kings 2:12.) These spiritual sons wanted their fathers' compassion, their heart for God, their love for the people, and their driving desire to please God.

Leaders of today need to learn what it means to honor their fathers. The word *honor* means "respect and esteem shown to another....the recognition of one's right to great respect or to any expression of such recognition"; "HOMAGE," which "adds the implication of accompanying praise"; "REVERENCE," which "implies profound respect mingled with love, devotion or awe"; "DEFERENCE," which "implies a yielding or submitting to another's judgment or preference out of respect or reverence";[2] "adoration"; "deference," as "a display of courteous regard...for one to whom respect is due, by yielding to the person's status, claims, or wishes...."[3] To honor someone is to think highly of the person; to show respect in acknowledgment or appreciation of the person's high character, position, or achievement; to put the person's wishes and opinions above your own.

The dictionary definition above does not go far enough because when it comes to honoring our fathers, belief, trust, and faith must be added. In order to honor our spiritual fathers, we must believe in the vision God has given them; trust in their faithfulness, righteousness, integrity, and ability to carry out the call on their lives; and have faith in their anointing.

Honor comes from, and is directed back to, God. It has little to do with the person himself. We do not honor our father's personality but the reflection of God in him. Our honor is actually being bestowed upon the righteousness of God, as it manifests through the one sent to minister to us.

I believe that the direction in the Word of God to honor our fathers applies to our spiritual fathers as well. Failing to honor our fathers according to the Word is an act of disobedience that will produce doubt, strife, and unbelief in us. Ultimately, it will result in preventing biblical covenant blessings from coming to us.

We do not honor our father's personality but the reflection of God in him.

Each of us needs to make a quality decision to begin to honor our fathers in thought, word, and deed, as well as with our prayers, finances, and service. When we do, we will receive the benefits of their wisdom, their prayers, and their anointing in our lives. Not only that, but we will prevent disloyalty from penetrating our hearts and our ministries.

CHAPTER 9

Loyal to God First

While it is important that we not be disloyal toward people, especially our pastors and leaders, we must be even more guarded against disloyalty toward God. When God instructs us to do something, by His Spirit or in His Word, and the outcome of our obedience is different than we would expect, we should not question God's ways of doing things and become disloyal toward Him.

Nowhere do we read in the Scriptures that if we do what the Word of God tells us to do then all will be well. In fact, in many of the stories of both the Old and New Testaments, the opposite appears to be true.

For example, the Old Testament prophet Jeremiah was called to preach a message *that would never be received.* Could you or I do that? Could we let go of our own sense of accomplishment or human affirmation in order to follow God in such a seemingly hopeless endeavor?

Could you or I preach to someone who killed our brothers and sisters in Christ? The New Testament prophet Ananias was called to do just that, and his convert was called to a ministry of even greater difficulty. The Lord told Ananias to lay his hands on Paul so that he could receive his sight, for He had shown Paul "...how great things he must suffer for my name's sake..." (Acts 9:16). *The Message* says it like this: "...now I'm about to show him what he's in for—the hard suffering that goes with this job...."

Ministers of the Gospel know that following the call is not a simple task. It is not easy to keep a tender and soft heart and to keep from questioning God during tough times. However, it is vital that we remain loyal toward God whether the circumstances appear to validate the call or not.

I remember when I began to establish my ministry. I had been the youth pastor, the worship leader, and the principal of the Christian academy at my church. Then the Lord sent me out to preach His Word.

I can remember it as though it were yesterday. I could hardly contain my excitement at being let loose on the world. As I drove to my first preaching engagement in a town called Katanning, a country town in Western Australia, the still, small voice of the Holy

Spirit said to me, "Ian, you must preach whether or not people come to your services." I was so excited to be out at all that I never even considered for a moment that no one would come.

I arrived in the town, set up the hall, and waited, and waited, and waited. No one came. Then I remembered what the Lord had said. In obedience, I got up with my microphone and began to preach to the empty hall. For the next five days, I preached morning and evening to an empty hall.

When I got home that week, I was so embarrassed and disappointed that I could not go to church. I did not want to see all the people who loved me and wanted to know how it all went. What would I say?

For two more weeks I went to that town, and only two people came one night to hear me preach. I still preached morning and night to an empty hall. Three weeks of no people, no offering, no salvations, no healings, no gifts of the Spirit. Nothing.

I then went to the next town, Kojonup. This is the place where my father had been a pastor in the '60s and, most importantly to me, where I had given my heart to Jesus at seven years of age.

I preached morning and evening for a week, and nobody came.

The following week I went to a place called Corrigin and again preached morning and evening for a week to no one. Five weeks had gone by, and I was beginning to doubt what God had instructed me to do. My church and my family were questioning my actions; I had no money; and I was very much alone asking God, "What in the world is going on? They didn't tell me about this in Bible college."

With a heavy heart, I went to the next town, Narrogin. The Holy Spirit had been silent since asking me to preach no matter who comes or not, so I was not exactly an example of enthusiasm that Monday morning, the first day of scheduled meetings. Three days before, a friend of mine had helped me to do a letter-drop to advertise, but once again I found myself preaching to an empty hall.

By Friday morning, no one had come. I was heartbroken and at the end of myself. "God," I said, "what are You doing? Why are You doing this to me? My church, family, and friends think I'm crazy. What is the purpose in all this?"

I was an emotional heap. All I knew was what the Holy Spirit had told me to do. Like Paul, I had been given a forewarning of some suffering, but at the time it was not comforting to me.

When Friday evening came, I went to the hall and began to play the piano. All of a sudden, thirteen people came into the hall! I nearly fell off the piano stool to get to them so they wouldn't go back out the door seeing no one else there. That night I preached as though there were 13,000 people present. I had a wonderful time and received my first offering into my ministry—about thirty-five dollars.

I was so excited to have seen people in the service that I thanked God nearly all the way home that night. I was about two hours from home when the Holy Spirit spoke to my heart and said, "That is enough, Ian."

What? I thought. *I'm just warming up! Let me at 'em, Lord!*

"No," He said. "I can trust you now. I now know that you are not going to give up, and I am going to send you to Sydney to begin a work for Me." I hadn't known that I was being tested. I hadn't known that suffering would be a part of my call. However, just like Paul, I had been forewarned and prepared for what I would endure.

Incidentally, the people who came to that first meeting in Narrogin asked me to come to minister to them every month, and they eventually formed the first Charismatic church in their town.

I could have succumbed to the temptation of disloyalty and turned my back on God for taking me through such a terrible test. I was only thirty years old, and though I was eager to follow His call, preaching to empty halls was not my idea of preparation and Holy Spirit training. I could have begun to doubt God's

...just like Paul,
I had been
forewarned
and prepared....

leading and expressed doubt and unbelief to those around me. I could have questioned God's provision and vision for my life simply because things did not work out.

The Scriptures do not say that if we do God's will, all things will work out as we think they should. However, in the greater scheme of things, God will have His way with those who are willing to follow His plan, not their own.

The seeds of disloyalty could have taken root in my heart during those initial disheartening weeks of my ministry. I often wonder how many people could still love God and believe they are in the very center of God's will while ministering to empty halls. Thank God that exam is over and my heart is still in love with Jesus and I am still looking for a new adventure.

Since those days, my faithfulness and loyalty to Jesus have only grown and His faithfulness and loyalty to me have been revealed in precious and new ways. Be careful not to let things you don't quite understand fester and rankle in your spirit and grow into huge trees of disloyalty. Instead, keep your heart loyal toward God, and you too will increasingly see His loyalty and faithfulness in your life and ministry.

CHAPTER 10

Loyalty Protection Scriptures

The way to protect loyalty in our own hearts is to regularly meditate on the Word of God and His instructions for our lives. As we do, the Word corrects us, comes alive inside of us, and reveals to us where we need to make changes.

DON'T FIGHT BACK

Be as mindful of the other person's worth as you are of your own. Don't give special attention to celebrities and the wealthy, but recognize the unrecognized. Don't get conceited over what you know. Repay no one a put down for a put down. Think of those things that are good in your relations with all people. Do your utmost to live in harmony with everyone. My beloved family, when anyone mistreats you, don't be obsessed with getting even with him; just drop it. Remember the record: "Leveling things is my business," says the Lord. "I will equalize." "If your enemy is hungry, give him food; if he is thirsty, give him a drink. By your actions you will reveal the contradictions in his behavior." Do not be mastered by negative forces in the universe, but master them with positive action.

ROMANS 12:16-21
Ben Campbell Johnson[1]

When you have been hurt and betrayed by someone you have trusted, this scripture stands up and says, "Don't fight back." I first learned this passage of Scripture in sixth grade when my teacher, Mr. Rundle, made all of us in his class repeat it until we knew it by heart. The phrase I remember most from the *King James Version* is "recompense ['to give back, restore, return,'[2] in other words, to reimburse; to 'pay back'[3]] to no man evil for evil."

Numerous times over the years I have wanted God to repay my vengeance on another; however, this scripture has rebounded into my heart and quieted my mind. Verse 19 says, "Vengeance is mine; I will repay, saith the Lord." The Lord, not you or I, will repay. When we read and meditate on this passage of Scripture, it settles us, which allows the Spirit of God to do what is best according to the condition of the other person's heart.

GAIN WISDOM AND UNDERSTANDING

The following passage of Scripture is a good confession over our hearts and minds.

And the spirit of the Lord shall rest upon him, the spirit of wisdom and understanding, the spirit of counsel and might, the spirit of knowledge and of the fear of the LORD; and shall make him of quick understanding in the fear of the LORD: and he shall not judge after the sight of his eyes, neither reprove after the hearing of his ears: but with righteousness shall he judge the poor, and reprove with equity for the meek of the earth: and he shall smite the earth with the rod of his mouth, and with the breath of his lips shall he slay the wicked. And righteousness shall be the girdle of his loins, and faithfulness the girdle of his reins.

The Lord, not you or I, will repay.

ISAIAH 11:2-5

Meditating on key words and phrases from these scriptures will give you a heart that seeks the best and sees the best in every person you meet. When the Spirit of wisdom and understanding indwells you, you make better and more informed decisions on a daily basis. When you have fair judgment, you will not judge by what you see or hear but by righteousness. As a result, you will become a faithful person.

HANDLE ANGER PROPERLY

Be ye angry, and sin not: let not the sun go down upon your wrath.

EPHESIANS 4:26

The Message version of Ephesians 4:26-27 says it all:

> *Go ahead and be angry. You do well to be angry—but don't use your anger as fuel for revenge. And don't stay angry. Don't go to bed angry. Don't give the Devil that kind of foothold in your life.*

> When the Spirit of wisdom and understanding indwells you, you make better and more informed decisions....

It is a manifestation of maturity to not let anger reveal itself. The scripture clearly tells us that there is a place for righteous anger; however, this is not an excuse to vent our own personal anger on someone. Confess this scripture, and be sure that you do not hold on to anything against any person after the sun has gone down.

BE UNFAZED BY RUMOR

> *No shuffling or stumbling around for this one, but a sterling and solid and lasting reputation. Unfazed by rumor and gossip, heart ready, trusting in GOD, spirit firm, unperturbed, ever blessed, relaxed among enemies.*
>
> PSALM 112:6-8 MESSAGE

I turn to this psalm when negative words have been spoken, or more subtlety implied, about me. As leaders, we must be sure to remain solid and level-headed during the times when we are verbally assaulted and discredited. In such times, I have read these verses and confessed that I would not be moved by unpleasant words. In those times, I ask the Lord to maintain my heart before Him, and He has always taken care of the situation for me.

WALK IN LOVE

Love endures long and is patient and kind; love never is envious nor boils over with jealousy, is not boastful or vainglorious, does not display itself haughtily.

It is not conceited (arrogant and inflated with pride); it is not rude (unmannerly) and does not act unbecomingly. Love (God's love in us) does not insist on its own rights or its own way, for it is not self-seeking; it is not touchy or fretful or resentful; it takes no account of the evil done to it [it pays no attention to a suffered wrong].

It does not rejoice at injustice and unrighteousness, but rejoices when right and truth prevail.

Love bears up under anything and everything that comes, is ever ready to believe the best of every person, its hopes are fadeless under all circumstances, and it endures everything [without weakening].

Love never fails [never fades out or becomes obsolete or comes to an end]....

1 CORINTHIANS 13:4-8 AMP

The truth in this passage of Scripture has great power to take care of not only you but the other person who is being used to bring pain to your heart. Walking in the love of God will turn your situation around more rapidly than any other action that you could take.

In the middle of controversy, it is not easy to still your heart and do what these verses suggest. For example, it is difficult to think the best of *every* person when one of them has just verbally assaulted you! However, the love of God in you can do it.

It is not easy to keep your heart soft and tender when certain churches will not give you the opportunity to minister the Word of God. Brother Copeland shared a story about a black preacher who was invited to preach in a church but was turned away when the elders discovered he was black. The preacher sat down on the steps outside the church and began to weep before the Lord, exclaiming, "Lord, You sent me here to preach, and they have closed the door to me and won't let me in." The Lord replied, "Do not worry about it, My son. They won't let Me in either, and I have been trying longer than you have."

Walking in the love of God will turn your situation around more rapidly than any other action....

That preacher laughed until it hurt, and then by the love of God he began to pray for the church. Soon, the church invited him back to preach and apologized for their actions. As a result, they had a precious outpouring of the Holy Spirit in their church.

Like that preacher, we have to practice the love of God when negative things are said and done against us. When we keep our hearts soft and tender, we will be able to seize the opportunity when God publicly restores our honor and integrity.

During challenging periods, perhaps of public disgrace, never forget how important it is to be accountable to a spiritual father.

Be found in the house of God every Sunday. This will stop pride and revenge from festering in your heart and life.

Remember that love pays no attention to a suffered wrong.

You are not alone: God is with you. Keep your heart open before Him and continue to walk in His love.

THE BEST IS YET TO COME

The best is really yet to come for you. When you have been going through a difficult time and you feel as though everyone is giving you a wide berth, it is important that you begin to meditate on the Scriptures. They will give you the courage to believe that God loves you and has not forgotten you, and other people of whom you are not even aware care for you also.

You do have a future and a purpose. Never allow the enemy to persuade you to take your eyes from the destiny that God has called you to fulfill.

> Let not mercy and truth forsake thee: bind them about thy neck; write them upon the table of thine heart: so shalt thou find favour and good understanding in the sight of God and man.
>
> PROVERBS 3:3,4

> I know the thoughts and plans that I have for you, says the Lord, thoughts and plans for welfare and peace and not for evil, to give you hope in your final outcome.
>
> JEREMIAH 29:11 AMP

> The boy Samuel grew and was in favor both with the Lord and with men.
>
> 1 SAMUEL 2:26 AMP

> You, Lord, will bless the [uncompromisingly] righteous [him who is upright and in right standing with You]; as with a shield You will surround him with goodwill (pleasure and favor).
>
> PSALM 5:12 AMP

> Even as [in His love] He chose us [actually picked us out for Himself as His own] in Christ before the foundation of the world, that we should be holy (consecrated and set apart for Him) and blameless in His sight, even above reproach, before Him in love.

For He foreordained us (destined us, planned in love for
us) to be adopted (revealed) as His own children through
Jesus Christ, in accordance with the purpose of His will
[because it pleased Him and was His kind intent].

EPHESIANS 1:4,5 AMP

You and I were not a mistake or a blunder. God purposely created us and gave us a destiny on this earth so that we would be constantly fulfilled while completing our assignment for Him.

Do not let anyone tell you, as has been told me, "You are finished. You can no longer preach the Gospel. You have lost all your friends, so just accept it and get on with life." God is not finished with you or me. If we allow Him to have His way with us, we will accomplish and complete all that He has called us to do. There is much to be done. Let's forget the disloyalties of the past and look toward the great future that lies ahead when we remain in our ever-loyal God!

God purposely
created us and
gave us a destiny
on this earth....

93

CHAPTER 11

Steel Convictions

My father shared many principles with me before he went on into the presence of his Master. These simple principles have guided my heart throughout life and will continue to do so. In addition to these principles my father has shared with me, I have included principles that I have learned over the years about leadership.

I want to share these principles with you to assist you in maintaining a right spirit and heart before God and your fellow believers and friends, even in the midst of personal or public challenges.

> Your only purpose in life is to please Jesus. In pleasing Him, you will please those you really need to.
>
> *Ian Britza*

> Never forget that a flaw in your witness may be a death of a soul.
>
> *William Britza*

Never make a judgment on a person or ministry based on what you have heard, or worse, not seen for yourself.

William Britza

Comment is free, but facts are sacred.

William Britza

When given leadership, remember to lead like Jesus, not like world leaders or even leaders you love and respect. Just imitate Jesus, and you will make your own mark in this world and be affectionately remembered for it.

Ian Britza

When dealing with people from all walks of life, and especially in difficult and trying circumstances, simply ask yourself, "How would Jesus respond?"

Ian Britza

Never forget that what you are in the home is the real you.

William Britza

Endnotes

Chapter 1

[1] Ben Campbell Johnson, *Matthew & Mark—A Relational Paraphrase*, (Toccoa, Georgia 30577: A Great Love, Inc., 1978).

[2] Johnson, "Matthew & Mark," comments on Mark 4:14, p. 116.

[3] Johnson, comments on Mark 4:15, p. 116.

[4] Johnson, comments Mark 4:16.

[5] Johnson, comments Mark 4:18,19.

[6] Johnson, comments Mark 4:20.

[7] *Webster's Third New International Dictionary of the English Language Unabridged* (Springfield, Massachusetts: Merriam-Webster, Inc., 1993, principal copyright 1961), s.v. "disloyalty."

[8] Webster's International, s.v. "violate."

[9] Webster's International, s.v. "disloyal."

[10] Webster's International, s.v. "faithless," "**syn**...DISLOYAL."

[11] Webster's International, s.v. "faithless."

[12] Webster's International, s.v. "faithless."

Chapter 3

[1] Bathsheba was the daughter of Eliam (2 Sam. 11:3), and Eliam was the son of Ahithophel. (2 Sam. 23:34.)

[2] Webster's International, s.v. "acquaintance."

[3] *Langenscheidt's New College Merriam-Webster English Thesaurus* (New York, Berlin, Munich: Langenscheidt KG, 1998; Springfield, Massachusetts: Merriam-Webster, Inc., 1988), s.v. "acquaintance."

[4] James Strong, "Hebrew and Chaldee Dictionary" in *Strong's Exhaustive Concordance of the Bible* (Nashville: Abingdon, 1890), s.v. "acquaintance" in Psalm 55:13, entry #3045, "*yada`*," p. 47.

[5] Strong, "Hebrew and Chaldee Dictionary," s.v. "acquaint" in Job 22:21, entry #5532, "*cakan*," p. 83, "to be familiar with...."

Francis Brown with the cooperation of S. R. Driver and Charles A. Briggs, *The New Brown—Driver—Briggs—Gesenius Hebrew and English Lexicon: With an Appendix Containing the Biblical Aramaic* (Peabody: Hendrickson, 1979 by Jay P. Green, Sr.), entry #5532 vb. "be of use" or "service, benefit," "Jb 22²¹, be familiar with, know intimately..."

[6] Strong, "Hebrew and Chaldee Dictionary," s.v. "guide" in Psalm 55:13, entry #441, "_alluwph," p. 12, from #502, "_alph," "familiar; a friend," p. 13.

[7] R. Laird Harris, Gleason L. Archer, Jr., and Bruce K. Waltke, eds., *Theological Wordbook of the Old Testament* (Chicago: Moody Bible Institute of Chicago, 1980), s.v. "_allûp," entry #108b, Vol. 1, p. 47.

[8] Webster's International, s.v. "profane."

[9] *Webster's New World™ Thesaurus* 3d ed. (New York: Macmillan, 1997 Simon & Schuster), s.v. "profane."

[10] First John 4:8 and 16 tell us, "God is love" (*agape*). The types of actions that *agape* controls, urges, impels, and compels are seen in 1 John 4:8-16 and in 1 Cor. 13 (in which *agape* is translated as "charity" in KJV).

James Strong, "Dictionary of the Words in the Greek Testament" in *Strong's Exhaustive Concordance of the Bible* (Nashville: Abingdon, 1890), s.v. "love" in 1 John 4:8,16; "charity" in 1 Cor. 13:1-4,8,13; entry #26, "*agape*," p. 7.

Chapter 7

[1] Ben Campbell Johnson, *The Heart of Paul, Biblical Truth in Today's Language,* (Toccoa, Georgia 30577: A Great Love, Inc., 1976), p. 119.

[2] AMP.

[3] MESSAGE.

Chapter 8

[1] In this text, the word "father" speaks of a spiritual elder and the term "son" speaks of a spiritual disciple. These terms are not meant to be exclusive but to serve as a gender-neutral reference to both men and women elders and disciples.

[2] *Merriam-Webster's Collegiate Dictionary* 10th ed. (Springfield, Massachusetts: Merriam-Webster, Inc., 2000), s.v. "honor."

[3] Webster's Thesaurus, s.v. "honor."

Chapter 10

[1] The Heart of Paul, pp. 38, 39.

[2] W. E. Vine, "An Expository Dictionary of New Testament Words" in *Vine's Complete Expository Dictionary of Old and New Testament Words* (Nashville: Thomas Nelson Inc., 1996), s.v. "RECOMPENCE, RECOMPENSE," p. 513, "B. Verbs," "2," #591. Used by permission of Thomas Nelson, Inc.

[3] NASB.

Prayer of Salvation

God loves you—no matter who you are, no matter what your past. God loves you so much that He gave His one and only begotten Son for you. The Bible tells us that "...whoever believes in him shall not perish but have eternal life" (John 3:16 NIV). Jesus laid down His life and rose again so that we could spend eternity with Him in heaven and experience His absolute best on earth. If you would like to receive Jesus into your life, say the following prayer out loud and mean it from your heart.

Heavenly Father, I come to You admitting that I am a sinner. Right now, I choose to turn away from sin, and I ask You to cleanse me of all unrighteousness. I believe that Your Son, Jesus, died on the cross to take away my sins. I also believe that He rose again from the dead so that I might be forgiven of my sins and made righteous through faith in Him. I call upon the name of Jesus Christ to be the Savior and Lord of my life. Jesus, I choose to follow You and ask that You fill me with the power of the Holy Spirit. I declare that right now I am a child of God. I am free from sin and full of the righteousness of God. I am saved in Jesus' name. Amen.

If you prayed this prayer to receive Jesus Christ as your Savior for the first time, please contact us on the Web at **www.harrisonhouse.com** to receive a free book.

Or you may write to us at:
Harrison House
P.O. Box 35035
Tulsa, Oklahoma 74153

About the Author

Ian M. Britza is an anointed minister of the Gospel who preaches the Word of God without compromise in a direct yet simple manner. He readily expounds upon profound truths gained from a lifetime of firsthand experiences—from his young beginnings as the son of a Baptist missionary and pastor to his roles of husband, father, pastor, and psalmist.

God has given Ian a very strong anointing to minister to pastors, leaders, and families. He especially ministers on the marriage relationship, parenting, and the training and correction of children. He has a powerful ministry to young people and is very candid in his teachings on biblical principles affecting teens—including dating, friendships, and right relationships.

After recording an album of quiet piano worship, he has been received as a gifted and talented musician with a precious anointing that ministers directly to the hearts of those listening as he plays the keyboard.

Pastor Britza has pioneered two churches in Australia, one in Sydney, New South Wales and in Brisbane, Queensland. He is President of Ian Britza Ministries Ltd. and hosts a weekly television program. He is a regular speaker at leadership conferences and youth ministries across Australia and the United States and now concentrates most of his time ministering in churches. Ian and his wife, Penny, currently reside in Perth, Western Australia.

To contact Ian Britza Ministries,

please write:

Ian Britza Ministries

P. O. Box 1606

Fremantle, 6959

Western Australia

or visit him on the Web at

www.ibministries.org

Please include your prayer requests

and comments when you write.

Other Books by Ian M. Britza

Christian Relationships and Dating
How To Coach Your Kids Through the Game of Life

Additional copies of this book
are available from your local bookstore.

www.harrisonhouse.com

Fast. Easy. Convenient!

- ◆ New Book Information
- ◆ Look Inside the Book
- ◆ Press Releases
- ◆ Bestsellers

- ◆ Free E-News
- ◆ Author Biographies
- ◆ Upcoming Books
- ◆ Share Your Testimony

For the latest in book news and author information, please visit us on the Web at www.harrisonhouse.com. Get up-to-date pictures and details on all our powerful and life-changing products. Sign up for our e-mail newsletter, *Friends of the House,* and receive free monthly information on our authors and products including testimonials, author announcements, and more!

Harrison House—
Books That Bring Hope, Books That Bring Change

The Harrison House Vision

Proclaiming the truth and the power
Of the Gospel of Jesus Christ
With excellence;

Challenging Christians to
Live victoriously,
Grow spiritually,
Know God intimately